HOST FAMILIES WANTED

Written & compiled
by Victoria Seymour

First published in 2006
By Victoria Seymour

Copyright Victoria Seymour.

Email: mail@victoriaseymour.com
Website: www.victoriaseymour.com

ISBN: 0-9543901-5-6

Printed in Great Britain by

impression IT.
Unit 7, Moorhurst Road,
Conqueror Industrial Estate,
St Leonards on Sea,
East Sussex
TN38 9NA
www impressionit.co.uk

This book is dedicated to the host families of Hastings and St Leonards.

My sincere thanks to the following student hosts who contributed their personal stories to this book

'Mr T S'. 'Mr B'. Val Relfe. 'Nettie'. Kay Green. 'Donna'. Cris Kennard. Olive Peddlesden. Mrs James. Bernadette James. 'Phillip'. Alan Notman. 'Stella Frances'. 'Mrs A' .

Information and research sources.

Hastings Borough Council.

Hastings Public Library Research Services.

Naomi Gotts.

June Brogger.

Joyce Brewer.

David Judge.

Noel Care.

Services to the author by Earlyworks Press.
www.earlyworkspress.co.uk

The cross-stitch cottage picture on the cover was designed and made by Wendy Johnson.

CHAPTER ONE

DO YOU SPEAK ENGLISH?

At three o'clock on a warm July morning in the early 1970s I was standing in my nightdress in the inner porch of our Victorian semi. In front of me was a small, androgynous person of Latin origin. I had been told to expect the arrival a 16-year-old Spanish girl but this little creature looked like a tired and nervous 12-year-old boy.

I asked as on scores of previous occasions, 'Do you speak English?' The response was a shrug and a sigh.

'Are you hungry or thirsty?' I asked.

The person looked desperate and after a few moments of thought brightened and said, 'I theenk ees Friday.' Followed by an obviously rehearsed, 'I am Mercedes; I am your student girl.'

I knew then I was in for another month of frustration, misunderstandings, miming and I hoped, laughter, until she had some grasp of English.

I took her suitcase and led her up to her bedroom. Not worth me going to bed now, the two German girls I was hosting were getting up at 4.00am to get on their departure coach.

At this time the overseas student industry, as we have since learned to call it, was approaching its height in Hastings and St Leonards. In the summer thousands of mostly European and Scandinavian students were accommodated with widely differing local families and given courses in English language at schools operating to widely differing standards. I began my work as a hostess to overseas students in 1964 after we bought a five bed-roomed house. Like many Victorian houses ours had undergone various conversions and extensions but I particularly liked the fact that there were still two sitting rooms, thus giving a quiet place for my daughters' homework sessions or for

1

receiving visitors away from the family turmoil. The kitchen/diner seemed huge; its main attraction was a large bay window with a low, broad sill that provided extra seating for the people who always seemed to congregate in the kitchen. Our change from renting to buying meant I had to find a job, but what? My two daughters were still at primary school and I had no qualifications; neither did I have much confidence for work outside the home. I was already helping my husband with the clerical work that was part of his job and the family and house absorbed the rest of my attention. Apart from an old vacuum cleaner I had no mod cons, all meals were home-cooked and the shopping done daily, on foot. My husband had persuaded me to learn to sew and knit and I made my own and my daughters' clothing, rather inexpertly in my opinion but it took up a great deal of time.

It was probably from the local newspaper that I learned about boarding overseas students; the adverts usually ran: 'Host Families Wanted'. Apart from a ten year old French girl, who spent a term at my school in Chislehurst in 1946 and two German prisoners of war who worked on a farm in the late 1940s with my father at Fairlight, I had no experience of foreigners. We made an application to one of the local language schools and our home was vetted by its owners. These were a local man and his German-born wife. The inspection of the house was thorough and we were allocated one student - a German girl, aged sixteen. Only one student you may ask - in a house with three spare bedrooms? But this was in the days before foreign students were brought into the town in hordes by the big student organisations. The founding idea of the arrangement, that the student's visit was a cultural exercise and not a profit making enterprise still prevailed in the 1960s. For our first student we were paid £7 per week and from this we had to provide accommodation, laundry, room cleaning and three proper meals a day. We were also expected to include the student in our family activities and entertainment when her half-day schooling was over. We were sent details of the student's visit well in advance of her arrival, giving us time to exchange family photographs and letters with her and her parents.

Our biggest initial expenditure when we decided to host overseas students was on furniture and bed linen. We bought two brand new single beds complete with mattresses that cost £25 each. For the bedroom suite we went to Papworth's, a second hand furniture shop in Hastings Old Town Courthouse Street. It was a rambling collection of warehouses, where pieces of massive Victorian and Edwardian furniture, despised in the early 1960s, were stacked in ramshackle piles, like scrapped cars. We found among these dinosaurs a modern, dark oak Old Priory bedroom suite with linen-fold detail for £20. Our house was still rather under-furnished so we bought a hefty mahogany roll-top desk for £6.00, a four-and-a-half feet high mahogany chest of drawers for £5.00 and an oak art nouveau sideboard with back mirror and prettily glazed cupboards for £4.00 and a pair of matching carver chairs for £2.00 each. These pieces of furniture had increased by many times their second hand purchase price when I sold them in 1982. Cotton bed sheets were expensive so we chose the cheaper option of fitted Bri-nylon sheets and frilled pillowcases in primrose yellow - dreadful things. They were hot in summer, chilly in winter and created enough static to almost catapult the sleeper from bed. A special, summer offer of 'Whitney' woollen blankets from Plummer Roddis (now Debenhams) and pale yellow tufted candlewick bedspreads, very fashionable then, completed the bed linen. We did not provide a desk or work table in the room as is requested today; most students seem to prefer to sprawl on their beds to write and read.

Our gas boiler was decrepit and inadequate for the size of the house; there was never enough hot water and I often had to resort to boiling kettles and pots for washing up and the family ablutions. The house had two toilets, both separate from the bathroom, a blessing when I was later housing four students, in addition to my own family of five. The ground floor toilet, damp and chilly, we kept for family use and the one on the south-facing landing was for visitors. What this toilet gained in the way of the sea view and a sunny aspect was lost to a temperamental cistern that would respond only to those trained in its uses. To the inexperienced, the toilet chain seemed to demand the timing and skill of a professional bell ringer. Advice on how to manipulate the flushing system, shouted at a new student through the closed toilet door, either by a family member or fellow students, served as an ice breaker or a source of acute embarrassment. A poverty of English language on the student's part or any foreign words for plumbing on ours was a great disadvantage. I feel certain that 40 years on, the toilet at that house is occasionally a topic at dinner tables in

France, Germany, Italy, Spain, Belgium, Sweden, Denmark and Finland, as my former students, probably grandparents by now, acquaint their families with the horrors of English plumbing.

Our very first student was Sabine from Düsseldorf. She arrived dressed in a little cream suit with a boxy jacket and a pill box hat in the Jackie Kennedy style and we treated her like a visiting celebrity. She was very organised; when complimented on her appearance she said that she had brought with her enough clothing and accessories to wear something different for each day of her month's stay and that she planned to keep a list of every meal she consumed in my house to show to her mother. This alarmed me, as cooking was not my forte and my wartime and austerity knowledge of ingredients meant that 'plain' was about the highest praise that could be given to my cuisine. These were days when the only kind of garlic you could buy in Hastings was a jar of stale-smelling garlic granules, olive oil was stocked solely by the chemist, for medicinal purposes; foreign food was regarded as 'greasy muck' by most British people. On tasting our bland sausages Sabine asked, 'Is bread?' We grew as close to her as her Teutonic aloofness would allow and my husband insisted that no expense should be spared in accommodating and entertaining her, with the result that the exercise left us out of pocket. On one occasion we did see Sabine's composure crack, when she returned from the town very distressed. She had been sitting on a wall by a bus stop with her friends when an old lady came out of a house and told the 'filthy Germans' to get off her wall, adding, 'The only good German is a dead German', it was a common wartime utterance here. To Sabine, who was born after the war was over, it was all history and she felt no responsibility for it, forgetting the old lady may have lost loved ones to the war. Similarly Sabine was dismayed by the amount of WWII films on British TV and the depiction of German soldiers as brutal monsters.

When she went home there were tears from my daughters and me but Sabine remained composed. A few weeks after she left we received a heavy parcel from Germany. It contained joints of smoked ham and pork and several types of German sausage. One was speckled with yellow mustard seeds and had an irresistible flavour that I could not identify. I discovered later it was proper garlic! The meats had come from Sabine's uncle who was a pork butcher in Düsseldorf. I could imagine them saying, 'Ve vill show zeez Englanders vot ist sausage!'

Apart from the old lady's hostile remarks about Germans, as far as I know Sabine was not exposed to street crime against overseas students. It was not common in Hastings in the 1960s. Sabine's departure in early August prevented her from witnessing violence of another kind in the town. From Easter 1964 the South East coastal seaside resort became a gathering place on Bank Holidays for Mods and Rockers, two groups of young road users. The Mods wore Parkas and neat suits were well groomed and rode Lambrettas, the Italian motor scooters. The Rockers, wild-looking men clad in leathers and knee boots rode powerful motorbikes. In the Easter and Whitsun Mondays of 1964 they converged on Brighton and Clacton and waged street and beach warfare on each other; often inflicting damage on the locals' persons and properties, resulting in arrests by the hundreds and group appearances in magistrates' courts. On 14th August 1964 it was the turn of Hastings to be the venue for what was dubbed, 'The Second Battle of Hastings' but this time the law was ready for them. Extra police were flown in from Northolt and with the local force they went to the Hastings seafront and beaches en masse and confronted the would-be adversaries and gave them the choice of either leaving or being arrested. A column of those who protested were taken out of the town on a route march, all uphill, to Fairlight and back again. Some offenders appeared in court the next day, where the sitting magistrate called them "Sawdust Caesars", a rebuke that became the title of a book about the Mods' and Rockers' seaside riots. In 2002 Hastings Museum mounted an exhibition of the clothing and vehicles and press cuttings telling the story of these now ageing miscreants. I thought the exhibition was too soon and in poor taste, in a town that had more than its share of street violence. The late Adam Faith, the singer who was a sartorial and musical icon to the Mods, opened the exhibition. As for the Rockers, their blitz on Hastings is now commemorated by their noisy but civilized arrival in Hastings by the thousands every early May Bank Holiday Monday. After parking up in neat rows, they mingle in peaceful harmony with hundreds of male Morris dancers who are dancing, while waving hankies and ribbons and jingling their little bells. Hail the New Man! Now that is a sight I would have dearly loved to have shown to Sabine.

In the sixties, the overseas student influx was mainly a summer phenomenon so I was obliged to look elsewhere for a wage for the rest of the year. I took a job that was euphemistically described as "School Dinner Supervisor" at Red Lake Primary School. I was not employed to supervise the catering but to oversee the children during their one and a half hour mid-day break. There were two sittings for the meals and it was required that four of the dinner-time team of six supervisors should watch over the diners while the two others patrolled the playground and kept order between the 100 or so children who were either awaiting their meal or had been fed. Should it be raining, the playground ladies had to take the mob into the school hall and read stories to them. If a member of the team were absent it was likely that there would only be one woman sorting out the boys' fights, sticky-plastering the grazed knees and changing the wet pants of this playground throng. Why it was considered that children who were eating a two course meal needed more supervision than the outdoor tearaways I could never understand. I grew close to some of the children, who liked to hold the "dinner lady's" hand as she patrolled. As we walked they talked, innocently revealing details of home life that were funny, tender and occasionally, heartrending. After the children had returned to lessons the child - supervising team and the catering staff had their meal in the school canteen, the same food that the children had eaten. It was food to gladden the heart of Jamie Oliver. Everything was cooked from basic ingredients, with plenty of fresh vegetables and visibly 'real' meat and fish. The steamed and milk puddings, sweet tarts and custard were delicious – my poor waistline! The working hours fitted in well with my own children's school timetable but the job was not well paid and so after two years I had to look elsewhere. I obtained a post as a welfare worker at the Ore Village education authority day school for chronically ill and physically disabled children and teenagers. Again a job with a misnomer; I was really a housemother, as most of the work was of this sort. The school had about 30 pupils but as many of them were ill and frail, a full complement was rare. During my time on the staff I became pregnant. I was 35 and with two daughters now in their teens and thought that my child-bearing time was over. While my condition was still a secret, the school's visiting nurse, who had come to talk to the three teenaged girls in the school about health and beauty, called me to the classroom to show my make-up-free face to demonstrate that cosmetics are not essential to have a good skin, (I was glowing with early pregnancy). Mentioning my fondness for fruit and vegetables, the nurse said, 'You see girls; it's not what you put on your face but what you put inside you that gives you a good complexion!'

I left the job when I was five months pregnant as the doctor thought I should not continue the lifting and carrying of heavy children that was part of the job, particularly because I was considered elderly in childbearing terms. After my son's birth at Christmas 1969, I reconsidered my potential as a wage-earner and hosting students offered itself again as the only viable choice. Much had changed in the overseas student business in the time that I had been absent from it. Language schools had sprung up all over the town, summer students were arriving in Hastings and St Leonards in their thousands and the arrangement of local families hosting students was beginning to be viewed as more of a commercial than an altruistic arrangement. That is not to say that the payments to the families were particularly generous. I think it was nine pounds a week. A French student, still only a single booking, came to me just before Easter, 1970. German and French students tended to arrive in the town about two or three weeks prior to the holiday, departing before Good Friday. My husband had insisted that if I was going to host students they must be female, mainly because we had teenage daughters and also because he said he would find male adolescents difficult to tolerate about the house. So we welcomed flame-haired, 18 year-old Isabella from Paris, for a two-week stay. Isabella was Jewish and her reason for wanting to improve her appalling English was to qualify for admission to a Kibbutz in Israel where her fiancé already lived. Her keenness to learn English extended beyond her half-day classes into every aspect of her and my life. She was at my side day and night and I could not even bathe or breastfeed my baby without her anxious face in front of me, asking questions on any subject, repeating the answer and demanding pronunciation tuition. She was fiery in nature and politics. I have no idea how we got on to the question of the torture of prisoners in Israeli goal one mealtime, but Isabella leaped from her chair, angry tears pouring down her face shouting, 'How dare you think that Israelis would torture anybody!' In those days I knew almost nothing about international political matters but decided thenceforth to keep the subject off the English conversation agenda. I had a postcard from

Isabella some months later, postmarked Israel, telling me she was living in a Kibbutz.

Although stereotyping is frowned upon in these politically correct times, a tendency towards national characteristics does exist: My German student girls seemed to be cool in temperament, more efficient and organised than the Italians and Spanish, many of whom were warmhearted, noisy and unpunctual. The Spanish also had a reputation as being the worst students of English, which was often true, in my experience. The Scandinavians generally had liberal views and a casual attitude to nudity, the girls sometimes startling my husband on the landing, as they emerged naked from the bathroom on their way back to their bedroom. And the Finnish do tend to be gloomy. I particularly enjoyed hosting groups of students of several nationalities; their lack of a mutual language forced them to speak English in the house and I loved the idea of having my own little United Nations around the table, especially when the offspring of former WWII enemies sat down together. Less altruistically, a mixture of nations was better for me, as isolation from their compatriots prevented the girls from ganging up on me or forming a ghetto within the household.

Most students brought me a gift. I amassed quite a collection of those little Swedish horses, either of orange-painted wood or glass and other glass ornaments; Sweden is famous for its glass manufacture. From elsewhere I was presented with small items of household linen, kitchen novelties, food and ingredients that were typical of the student's country and a shelf-full of knick-knacks of every kind. The girls' attitudes on arrival differed widely: Some were brimming with excitement, ready to embrace every aspect of the new experience. Some had been sent to England merely to get them out of their parents' hair in the school holidays; others had been press-ganged into the trip because their parents thought it would be good for them. These latter were usually miserable and homesick. On her arrival one 17-year-old Italian girl dumped her suitcase in the hall, demanded to use the telephone and in floods of tears begged her parents to let her go back to Italy at once. They refused but after a few days of grief and hostility the girl settled down and had a very happy stay, shedding tears of sadness on leaving us. A spoilt 14-year-old Austrian girl from a very rich background despised me, my family and our modest home from the start. Her pleas to her parents to let her go home were rejected so she drew a 28-day grid and hung it in her bedroom, marking each passing day with a big X, meanwhile creating havoc in my household with meddling and complaints.

We began hosting students when my daughters were still in secondary school and our two young daughters were rather in awe of these foreign girls, who had lots of pretty clothes, wore makeup and were allowed a freedom still beyond their sheltered existence. Later, my daughters' attitudes began to change. The elder, B. became resentful of the students; this was expressed in hogging the bathroom at key times of the day or peering mistrustfully at her plate during family mealtimes, thus wilting the appetite of a newly arrived student. It would be unfair to her to say that this was a constant state of affairs. On occasions B would have the students in helpless laughter, as she read their mother-tongue books in her own version of the correct pronunciation of the language. I had no idea that here was a hint of my daughter's eventual career. My younger daughter, T, just withdrew to her room, relieved each year when the student season was over. To my little son it was all great fun; a repeated renewal of a collection of temporary big sisters. Some students had younger siblings whom they were missing, so they were pleased to use my son as a substitute. When he was a baby the Italian girls would take him naked from his bath and pop him into their beds while they pranced around, cooing at him and trying on clothes for a night out. I imagined that one day he would say of this, "Why do the right things happen at the wrong time?" (He did). From the age of about five he began to learn foreign card games from the students and the more tomboy-ish took him for a football kick-about, in the field at the back of Sandown School, opposite to our house. Some people think that boys who are raised with sisters have a better understanding of women when they are men. Put scores of temporary sisters into the equation and imagine the effect!

My husband encouraged me in the hosting of students in principle; it enabled me to be at home for the children and available to give him on-the-spot secretarial help with his business. In practice it was less agreeable. He was a reserved but dutiful man and undertook his role of being *in loco parentis* seriously but the arrangement encroached on his privacy to a considerable degree. After a few years the chattering and constant comings and goings of students began to be difficult for him to bear but he insisted I carry on with the work. It was clear that in my husband's yearning for peace he was not alone. Most mornings in the summer months, I would see my neighbour's husband cross the road to a patch of woodland, mug of tea in hand, to escape the breakfast turmoil in his own student-occupied household. Eventually my husband installed a small, secondhand caravan in the garden and equipped it for his use as an office, which also provided a useful bolt hole for me.

I imagine that some host mothers find that her children and husband can become rather fed up with the amount of time given to the students. For me it was difficult to draw the line between proper care and over-indulgence; I was always worried that I was not doing quite enough for the students and as a result, was most probably doing far too much. The students would often engage me in long conversations, with a bit of English homework help on the side. It was however a two-way thing; I learned much from these girls; how similar to ours, yet fascinatingly different, are the lives of the people in other countries. We discussed family relationships, food, customs, education and entertainment and I formed an understanding of daily life in foreign countries that years of tourist holidays could never have provided.

The majority of my students were adolescent but occasionally I would host adult females who had come to improve their English, often to advance their careers. And what a joy they were! They had outgrown the usual teenager's careless acceptance of all that is done for them and were grateful for every small service, at times they even helped out! I recall with particular fondness two plump Mexican businesswomen, who came home from every school excursion with an amusing gift for me, presented with laughter, hugs and kisses. A Japanese woman, aged 26, had us all worried; she never instigated conversation and kept standing up every time my husband came into the room. We learned that when a Japanese woman is a guest it is considered very impolite for her to start a conversation and her rising to her feet was out of respect for the head of the household. She looked miserably uncomfortable on western furniture, accustomed as she was to kneeling while eating and to sleeping on a mattress on the floor. I had to coax these facts out of her, as she never complained – too polite! She did unbend sufficiently to put on her national dress, a process that took a very long time but she emerged from her bedroom a vision in yellow-gold satin.

With the increase in numbers of overseas students in the town the language schools were keen to find families who could accommodate students in pairs or even three or four at a time. By 1972 I was hosting a quartet of foreign girls at the peak of the season. For some language schools the idea that the family accommodation of overseas students was a purely cultural scheme was scarcely acknowledged but like most hostesses I tried to give language help to the students, along with the mothering of all the people under my roof. That summer my elder daughter became 17; she had just started work at the Hastings Observer and her father agreed that she could go out in the evenings with our students. On the evening of her first outing, the hour after supper was full of excitement; five teenage girls trying on outfits and trying out make-up.

During that evening the plan to protect our daughters from contact with foreign boys was undone. B met an Italian, M, and he was entranced by her long golden hair, blue eyes and petite figure. He walked her home at 10.30pm, her 'Cinderella' hour, with all the student girls as escorts. The Italian, almost 18, was persistent in his attentions and within a few days my husband heard about him and he was not pleased. My other daughter and I persuaded him to take a lenient view and after subjecting the boy to a lecture straight out of a Victorian melodrama, my husband allowed the friendship to continue, regarding it as a mere holiday fling. My elder daughter was not the only one in the household enmeshed in a cross-nationality romance. Each one of my four student girls had paired up with a boy from elsewhere, the Italian with a Swede, the German with a Spaniard and the Spanish girl had met Japanese boy who took her fancy. Most worrying was the Swedish girl; she was 14, confident, statuesque and sophisticated, she looked about 21; she was spending her out-of-school time with a 23-year-old English man, who was on holiday in Hastings. We reported the liaison to the school, who regarded the matter as trivial, so my husband took the Englishman aside and gave him another version of the Victorian lecture, but as the departure of all the students was imminent, we knew the problem would resolve itself naturally. The night before they left my students stayed awake, sitting in my kitchen-diner till dawn, some of them weeping intermittently, while my daughter and the Italian held hands and looked distraught. We imagined that with his return to Italy the romance was over but we had not reckoned with the determination of this Romeo. Immediately following his return to Milan the phone calls and letters began and M came to spend Christmas of that year with us. Return hospitality for our daughter was offered by M's parents for the following Easter holiday. Our daughter's wages were low and my husband refused to give her the money for the flight, saying that if she really wanted to go she must find the money herself. So she took an after-work job as a cleaner and well before Easter had enough for the air fare. Then her father gave her the money for the flight as she had proved her determination and he told her to use her earnings as emergency or pocket money. Of course we were both worried at her going abroad alone and for the first time. But had we not welcomed into our house girls from overseas who were three or four years younger than her?

B returned ten days later full of her new experiences. She told us about the Italian family, their life and cuisine. She brought home dried herbs, basil and oregano, and pasta, fresh garlic, a block of Parmesan cheese, dark green olive oil, the fragrant cake, panettone, and a jar of tomato sauce made by M's mother. B taught me the proper way to cook pasta and how not to swamp spaghetti with great dollops of sauce but to use just enough to coat the strands. As she recounted her adventures I thought that this is how my students must have returned to their own countries but I doubted that they took back such tasty gifts. I recall one German girl who took home a jar of Marmite to show her family what disgusting food the British eat. As a general rule, most German students disliked the spread and were astonished to learn we put it on toast for babies and small children.

Talk with any student hostess and you are soon on to the subject of food. For one summer I was lucky to have some help on the kitchen front in T, my younger daughter. She took an after-school job in a farmhouse kitchen, a cottage industry run by a woman who grew up in a well known Sussex bakery family. T learned to make meat and fruit pies and cakes on a catering scale. She soon became adept and brought her skills home to help me in the kitchen. By then, hosting four students at a time during the height of the summer was normal for my household. Finding attractive menus to satisfy the hungry visitors and keep within a budget was a challenge. One summer I decided to experiment with 'high tea' for some of the evening meals; a light, cooked protein dish, cauliflower cheese, home made fish cakes or stuffed omelettes, followed by cakes and pastries. My own baking was of a poor standard and so my daughter stepped in. Once or twice a week we set about an old-fashioned baking afternoon, my daughter as chief cook, with me as assistant. My capable younger daughter turned out cakes and pastries with speed and efficiency: Fresh fruit tarts, zingy lemon meringue pies, rock cakes bursting with sultanas and candied peel, golden or chocolate fairy cakes, their sliced-off crowns bisected and set on the cake at a butterfly-wing angle, in a swirl of butter cream. Coconut cakes, the taste enhanced with a little almond flavouring were very popular. One afternoon a mistake in collecting the ingredients added a new dimension to this recipe. I put on the work-table peppermint flavouring instead of almond and the cakes were made and in the oven before I realised the error, so we served them up anyhow. They were a hit and became a standard. A popular cake that my daughter made was a plain, six-portion scone round, sliced in half and filled with vanilla flavoured cream, in which fresh strawberries had been crushed. The top of the scone was decorated with a dusting of icing sugar, whole strawberries and their leaves. When the students came home, the house was filled with the aroma of baking. The girls would sit on the wide window sill of the bay window in my kitchen and tell me about their day, while admiring the racks of cooling cakes and pastries. The students loved the high tea days, a very unhealthy meal by today's standards. One very beautiful slender girl, of mixed Polynesian, French, Italian and Spanish descent, put on six kilos during her stay and could not fasten her designer jeans. My daughter, not much more than a child felt she had done enough baking sessions, so they came to an end. But those cooking afternoons remain as a most happy memory for me. My daughter eventually became the cook in the restaurant at a complex for retired people.

One of the unfortunate consequences of the heavy English diet on the students was the onset of constipation. (The least afflicted seem to be the Germans, who were used to heavy food and also tended to bring their own "pharmacy"). The saddest victims from this distressing complaint were the Italians. It is not without reason that Italy is known as the Garden of Europe; for the most part its population eat an abundance of fruits and vegetables, and of course, always olive oil. Deprived of this lubricant the girls were soon 'bloccato', as they said.

For me, one of the disadvantages of student hosting was that I was hardly ever off duty. My husband would not allow the students to have keys, so my excursions outside the house were confined to the hours the students were in classes or on school trips. As the years passed my daughters started work, one on rolling shifts and I was also accommodating students with staggered timetables so I found myself running an all day cafeteria to fit in with varying arrival and departure times.

Every hostess has an anecdote about sandwiches: The language schools eventually ended the arrangement of students returning to the host family for a mid-day meal. The students went directly from morning lessons to excursions or afternoon activities and the packed lunch became the norm, proving to be something of a nightmare. Most families used white cut loaves for sandwiches and these tasteless, damp slices were alien to the students. It may be said that today's sliced bread is probably even less wholesome. (Many overseas students, who are fed the mass-produced, sliced bread, find that within a few days they are suffering from stomach pain, bloating and embarrassing flatulence). What to put in the sandwiches was a constant challenge, bearing in mind that the food sat for a morning in a hot, summer classroom, inside a student haversack. Salad stuff wilted, cheese turned greasy, meat became a bit suspect and fish was unthinkable. Fresh fruit, cakes and crisps were the salvation of the lunch-pack. No wonder then that I was once told by somebody, who had been driving behind a fleet of coaches bearing students on an afternoon excursion, that the hedges were suddenly festooned with sandwiches jettisoned by the passengers. Most humiliating of all was to find the packed lunch, discarded in the student's bedroom waste-bin at the end of the day, both of us too shy to say anything. It would have helped if I had known then that the students preferred bread rolls and they did not spread butter on them.

In the mid-1990s I found myself on a rescue mission for students' packed sandwiches. Three students, who had no key and whose family was not home, sought sanctuary with me. They were hungry but still had their uneaten packed lunches; soggy sandwiches of sliced bread with cheese and tomato filling. I removed the filling from the bread and spread it with tomato puree, sprinkled it with dried basil and oregano, placed the tomato and cheese slices back on top of the bread and put each slice, cheese uppermost, under a hot grill until it was golden and sizzling. I called it pizza toast. Apparently this stop-gap snack, a favourite with my own children for years, became a legend among that year's students.

As time passed, it seemed that our daughter's relationship with M was set to continue and so I decided to learn Italian. After having had Latin and French crammed into me at grammar school it was not too difficult to learn Italian. In the phrase made famous by Manuel in Fawlty Towers, 'I learned it from a book', and in time could speak enough Italian to make myself understood. I tried it out on the Italian students and on M on his rare visits to England; it even came in handy with a few Spanish students who had almost no English at all.

After five years, consisting of long periods of separation for the young couple and hectic, brief reunions, M completed his university studies and military service and he and our daughter were to be married. The bridegroom's newly widowed mother and his brother were the only members of the family who were able to attend the wedding in Hastings in 1977. They stayed with us for their visit. The mother was enchanted with Hastings and said, according to M's translation, 'It is like a fairy-tale town, with a magic castle and sweet little houses up and down the rocks, each with its own garden.' How we locals go about with our eyes closed! The bridegroom's brother, who was 15, spoke some English but the mother none, so I struggled to get to know her with the aid of my home-learned Italian. She was very gracious, beautiful and elegant but her younger son was full of naughty tricks, the worst possible companion for my eight-year-old son who was already doing well in the mischief business himself. During the few days before the marriage the boys broke a bedroom window and the bridegroom's brother fell through the plastic roof of next door's summer house while in pursuit of a cat.

1946

The marriage was at St Mary Star of the Sea, a nuptial mass, said twice, once in English and then again in Latin; it was the longest service I have ever attended. The reception had elements of both countries; Spumanti not Champagne was served for the toasts and we became acquainted with the Continental custom of presenting guests with 'confetti'; this was not the throwing of showers of paper fragments but distributing prettily wrapped packets of sugared almonds. The couple had a short honeymoon in the UK, returning to our house for a few days before leaving for their new home in Milan.

We continued hosting students until the late 1970's. During that time my husband's health began to deteriorate. After his death in spring 1980 I tried one more summer as a host mother; it was too soon. I buried my grief behind manic cheerfulness and constant activity. That season I hosted my first student from Saudi Arabia. She had my little attic room to herself, as she wanted a single room. I thought it was very cosy but it must have fallen short of her expectations and she complained to her father, who subjected me to an abusive phone call from Riyadh. All the suppressed fury I felt at my young widowhood surfaced and I let fly at him; he was reduced to near subservience. On seeing this, his daughter must have thought that I was a strong woman and so sought my help in a terrible situation. She said, "I have a problem." Those of you who have hosted students will know that this means, "You have a problem." My student had a friend in another host family who was about to a have an abortion just before her departure from Riyadh. Unexpectedly, her flight time was brought forward and the abortion did not take place. Could I arrange an abortion? The pregnant girl was engaged to be married and her fiancé was the father of her child. I saw no problem but my student said it was a great dishonour to the family and the pregnant girl's brothers and father would kill her and the fiancé. My questions to a Middle-Eastern acquaintance about Arab culture revealed that this was very likely. This situation was beyond me, I had no idea how to acquire an abortion and even if I had that information I would not have been party to arranging it. I handed the problem to the school's welfare officer, who calmly listened to the story, as if it was not the first time she had heard such a thing. She said, "Leave it to me." I heard nothing more, nor did I want to. I did think of the pregnant girl's host family who, if fate had not intervened, would have been accommodating an 18-year-old girl who had just undergone an abortion. I ended that student season hosting four 15-year-old girls from the same country. They were as quick to spot a broken person as a cat is to find an injured bird. They ganged up on me and were constantly spiteful. I decided to give up hosting. In truth I was burned out.

I sold the large house in which I had spent the greater part of my married life, bought a small bungalow and took up two voluntary occupations; one with a single-parent group and the other working shifts on a 24-hour telephone support line. I also set about 'finding myself', not as common then among middle-aged women as it is today.

My husband's health had prevented us from going to Italy to see our daughter, who was by 1981 the mother to a toddler and a babe in arms, both girls. I was very impressed with the way she had integrated into Italian life. She had gone to live in Milan in 1976 as an au pair a year before her marriage, to learn the language. Her work with the children was daunting: With no training in childcare she was left alone for many hours a day with a baby and toddler. Their home-coming parents were busy and tired, with little time to chat. So at first, B's Italian language was infantile, as the children were her main source of conversation. Later, she got an office job in a Milan language school. She worked hard to learn Italian and the many aspects of Milanese daily life; shopping, travelling around the city on public transport and coping with the convoluted bureaucracy of Italy, which was complex even before the event of the European Union. B's fiancé was, of course, never far from her side and it was a comfort to her father and me that she had his guidance.

My initial trip to Italy was the first time I had ever flown. As the plane rose over Gatwick I was transfixed with fear. My young son sitting at my side, held my hand tightly, to reassure *me,* not himself. He was enjoying every moment! People who hear that I have family living in Italy say, 'How wonderful', probably recalling lazy, sun-drenched Italian holidays and touring famous and beautiful cities and monuments. But visiting one's family is an entirely different thing; the demands of their everyday life must come first. Taking part in Italian domestic activities is an experience denied to the average tourist and a privileged way of getting to know Italy. I also thought that in a way I was on the receiving end of the student-host family situation. Shopping was a big adventure, the foods so different, fruits and vegetables far larger and more succulent looking than our own northern specimens and varieties of fish and cuts of meat that I had never seen before. I encountered beggars in the street for the first time and my heart was wrung by the sight of a scruffy woman, extending a pleading hand, while holding a dirty baby at her breast. My daughter urged me to walk on, saying that if I gave her money we would not get rid of her. My shocked and ignorant comment, 'Something should be done', at supper that night must have been irritating. Now we have beggars in the street in Hastings and I hurry past, mainly because I am nervous of them, suspecting they are drunk or on drugs.

B had already made quite a few friends in Italy and as the visiting grandmother I was welcomed into homes with generous Italian warmth and hospitality, especially by my son-in-law's mother, a superb cook and home-maker. During further visits to Italy my daughter and her husband made every effort to show me the Italy beloved by tourists. We went for a picnic in the hills outside Milan; we sat beside a shallow river, barbequed tiny fish and drank wine chilled in the water that flowed from the ice-capped mountains above. One evening my son-in-law took me to an open-air orchestral concert, in the piazza in front of Milan Cathedral. The soaring pinnacles of the cathedral, the soaring music of the orchestra and the warm evening sun made it a memorable occasion. Yet Philistine that I am, the memories are linked with the recollection of watching a flea struggling through the long dark hair of the elegant lady behind whom I sat. One hot afternoon we drove to an ancient monastery set amidst rice-fields in the broad River Po plain. The steps in front of the monastery's patron saint are worn away by centuries of pilgrims' feet. There were very few monks in residence, even in Italy the attractions of the religious life are fading. For several years my daughter and her husband had a home in Piacenza, a rural city, about one hour's drive from Milan. They occupied a top flat in what we would call a listed building, in the old part of the city. The flat overlooked the garden of the monastery attached to a cathedral and the days were punctuated by the ringing of the bells that ordered the monks' lives. I found that looking down on the tranquil comings and goings of the few monks remaining in residence was comforting to me, still at odds with my new role in life.

One year I was invited to Italy for the marriage of my son-in-law's brother, grown beyond chasing cats, to a girl from a farming family. I love weddings and this one was conducted in great style. After the marriage, in the church in a rural town, a cavalcade of cars decorated with streamers set off at speed, car drivers sounding their horns, passengers cheering, to assemble at a hillside restaurant. The wedding meal, a seventeen course affair, began in the afternoon and continued into the night. Endless toasts were proposed and honoured in potent, home produced wine. The old men drank their wine from soup bowls, in the Italian farmer's manner. In my prim, white boater hat and navy blue, white-spotted dress I became the butt of humour for the old uncles. I heard the name Mary Poppins bandied about. I too drank wine from a bowl and became past caring what they called me. Bawdy Italian songs were sung and lewd tricks and charades were performed by the younger guests, to the discomfiture of the bride and groom. It was all far removed from the formal and restrained reception after my daughter's marriage in Hastings.

It was in the mid-eighties that B's Italian neighbours, hearing her small children speak English, asked her if she would teach the language to their little ones. So she invented lessons as a form of play – word-games combined with physical activities. It seems my daughter is a natural teacher and the children made remarkable progress. Soon B was asked to take her learn-by-play scheme into her children's primary school and thereafter she was approached by other parents who wanted their older children to be given extra school tuition in English. My daughter took a course in teaching English to cope with the more sophisticated needs of the older students. She was then asked to teach groups that quickly grew in number and increased in ages until, in the early 1990s, the youngsters asked, 'Please will you take us to England for a summer holiday?'

CHAPTER TWO

MANOR, MANSION, CASTLE AND SEMI-DETATCHED.

In 1994 my daughter felt ready to bring a group of students to Hastings. She asked me to book the ferry, liaise with accommodation owners, to research the costs and times of Hastings' visitor attractions and to collect information on excursions to Brighton, Canterbury and London. I did this on an informal basis, a case of 'mum helping out'. In July, B brought to Hastings a group of 30 Italian students in their early teens by coach; a slow but pleasant way to travel, with none of the inconveniences associated with the cut-price, group air travel favoured by many schools. The students and their accompanying staff and chaperones stayed at Broomham Hall Boarding School at Guestling. It was the summer holidays and the boarders were on holiday. I had known of Broomham for many years but only as an interesting building, seen across a field, on journeys to and from Rye. It was always worthy of a longer look in spring, when closely planted daffodils and trees bearing pink almond blossom enlivened the long drive-way to the hall. The students not only boarded at Broomham but had lessons there; the coach that had transported them from Milan was used for their trips to Hastings and excursions around Sussex, Kent and to London.

Broomham, a former manor house, is in an idyllic setting in the midst of open parkland, with pitches for outdoor games and a swimming pool. The building, with a little round turret, dates from the 16th century and the interior reflects this historic origin, with brick-floored narrow passages to the lower rooms and a fine oak staircase leading to the upper floor. Of course, there has to be a ghost. Staff members said they have encountered a phantom woman, as she drifts along the passageway from the kitchen. She enters the building through an exterior wall, which is now a sunken garden, formerly part of a kitchen. The army occupied the building in WWII and knocked it about disgracefully, (standard behaviour). A Guestling resident, Stella Francis, remembers Mrs Mattingly who lived at Broomham after the war. 'She and her husband rented the property from the owners, the historic Ashburnham family. Mrs Mattingly was an Italian countess and she looked like the Duchess of York and dressed her daughters like the two royal princesses. Mrs M employed Italian girls as what would be called au pairs today but they did a lot of domestic work too, including making fresh pasta, which they laid out to dry in the big kitchen. During the war Mr Mattingly became Major Mattingly of the Guestling Home Guard.' In 1984 a Mr Jan Auer opened Broomham School in the premises. He was the headmaster and his mother Felicia was the Principal. By 1988 they had 70 boarders.

 The pupils' bedrooms in the early 1990s were furnished in the manner the British expect from boarding schools, a style that might be described as Utilitarian-Spartan: Bare board floors covered by threadbare rugs, wooden beds, some rickety from the attentions of their regular occupants, scant storage for possessions and battered writing tables. To me, raised on boarding school stories, it was delightfully atmospheric but not so to the students, who were accustomed to more comfort. Their protests seemed pretty hollow, when in the space of a couple of days the furnishings disappeared under the mounds of detritus that seems to be the universal décor of the teenager's bedroom. I thought that the food at Broomham was quite superior for a boarding school. The cook produced thrice-daily, freshly-cooked meals to warm the heart of any British school child - it was substantial and plenty of it. The Italians pined for pasta and olive oil but on this occasion they had to settle for the Broomham version of spaghetti Bolognese. In subsequent years my daughter brought supplies of pasta, olive oil and parmesan cheese, so that the residences where her students stayed could provide a taste of home to nostalgic students. Spoiling them? Of course she was. Her charges were well-known to her; she had taught most of them from early childhood and she knew their parents - parents she would have face immediately on their children's return from the UK. That prospect would sharpen anyone's sense of responsibility.

Although the young Italians were initially hostile to what they saw as the privations and isolation of Broomham Hall, they soon came to love the place and its cook, who adapted her English cuisine as best she could to suit a Latin palate. My daughter's birthday is in early July and because of her student trips she has frequently celebrated it in her home country. In 1994, my family and I took an evening picnic, with wine and a birthday cake out to Broomham, to celebrate with her. After dark I went out into the grounds, not troubled by the story of the resident ghost and stood in the middle of the football pitch, from where I viewed the night-sky, devoid of the light pollution that is ever present in the town. Rabbits scuttled away into a low-lying mist and the air was full of mid-summer scents and that indefinable fragrance we think of as country air. I wonder if the Italians of the class of '94 remember it like that.

The students' final departure from Broomham was one of typical Italian drama; much leaping off the coach for yet one more hug for the Broomham staff and then leaving with tearful, backward glances at their 'little English castle'. By the time the students reached Milan all memories of their initial dissatisfactions had faded and many of them were already eager to return to Hastings the next year. Certainly, the students we brought to Hastings in the summer of 1994, many of whom are now in their early thirties, look back on their first trip to England and living in a 'castle' with affection. For students that came in following years there was to be accommodation in an authentic, picture book-castle, with a moat and drawbridge.

The last student I ever hosted was Danielle, aged 19, who stayed with me in February 1995, under a personal arrangement. She was one of my daughter's private pupils and old enough to travel without a group. By then I had moved to a modest two-up, two-down mid-terrace cottage. Danielle came from a small Italian town where everybody knew everyone's business; even an absence from Sunday mass would be remarked upon. She relished the freedom that the two-week break in England would give her, particularly because her 20-year-old boyfriend was staying in a nearby host family. The fact that it was winter in no way spoiled their visit: They went to Hastings Old Town pubs at night to listen to live bands; they visited the local tourist attractions when their English lessons were over; when I had to go out in the evenings the boyfriend would visit Danielle to keep her company in my house. They must have had a blissful time! Danielle said that she wanted to eat only English foods during her visit, so I had 14 days to run through my repertoire of recipes. I cooked every variety of breakfast meal, the full English, kedgeree, kippers, eggs in every way and just about the most luxurious porridge possible, made with milk and served with thick cream. I gave Danielle a roast chicken

Christmas dinner with plum pudding and mince pies to follow, neck of lamb stew with pearl barley, liver and bacon, shepherd's pie, fish and chips, cod in parsley sauce and steak and kidney casserole. Dessert was essential to complete the English gastronomic experience; I served sherry trifle, bramble apple tart with custard, steamed sponge pudding, suet pudding with syrup and cold and hot milk puddings, Strangely, tapioca pudding, hated by British children, was a hit with Danielle. Perhaps the strawberry jam on the pudding helped. She loved British TV and on the nights she stayed in we would view together, with the Teletext subtitles switched on, to help improve her English. I spoiled her outrageously, as much for my own sake as hers. I knew she would be my last student guest and it was good to end my years as a hostess on such a happy note.

At about the same time my daughter decided to take a business partner into her student educational holiday scheme, a retired Italian headmistress. I was asked if I would continue to do the work formally that I had been doing on an informal basis. I had no real idea of the job I was taking on and probably neither did my daughter. The tasks built up gradually, usually prefaced with, "Could you possibly...?" or "Do you mind just...?" The Italian partner brought with her a new impetus and an intention to make the project more commercial. With her previous contacts in the Milanese education system she had access to a number of teaching establishments. My daughter's private pupils remained as clients of the scheme and did so throughout its existence, one of them coming back to Hastings for eight successive years. With the increase in student numbers, additional accommodation would be needed and the partners decided to find a new student residence as well as engaging Hastings host families. These were my first official jobs - to locate a big building, preferably a boarding school and to advertise for and inspect host family accommodation.

I do not recall from where I heard that Hurst Court on the Ridge was preparing to open as a residential student centre. To provide some background about the building I quote from my book, "The Long Road to Lavender Cottage", a part-history of the Ridge.

'Hurst Court School, once a boarding school for boys, stands on the corner of The Ridge and Chowns Hill. The school was built at the

behest of Doctor Reed of Dover. A transcript of an advert from the London Illustrated News dated 19th September 1868 describes the school as being run by Dr Martin Reed and states: 'The school receives the sons of gentlemen from the ages of 6-18 years. First class particulars and references are available on application'. A footnote to this record mentions that Hurst Court is reputed to be haunted by the ghost of a maid who, together with her child, died of a fall from the building. Apparently only the maid is seen, not the child. French Jesuit Priests occupied Hurst Court briefly from 1883 to 1887, having been expelled from their country. According to a contemporary report the priests found Hurst Court convenient for sea bathing as it was 'merely one hour's walk to a convenient bay'. The Jesuits moved on to new quarters at Hollington because the numbers in their community quickly outgrew the considerable accommodation at Hurst Court.

One boy who spent a brief and unhappy time at Hurst Court as a boarder was Gavin Maxwell, who in adult life wrote "Ring of Bright Water" and many other wildlife books. "Ring of Bright Water" sold more than a million copies and inspired one of the best loved British films of all time. Maxwell became an instructor for the Special Operations Executive during WWII. Hurst Court School for Day Pupils and Boarders eventually closed in 1968 and merged with the Belmont School at Hassocks. The reason given for the closure was the poor road and rail transport system between Hastings and London. Hurst Court was re-opened as a Conference Centre in 1970. Later, a local family, who had a care home, adapted the basement of Hurst Court to use as a day centre for the disabled, with a view to the rest of the building being put to other use.'

I went to look at Hurst Court on a particularly cold February day in 1995 and my student Danielle and her boyfriend came with me, just to have a new kind of 'English experience'. At that time most of the main building was under interior conversion, repair and refurbishment. Kevin Tomlin, a member of the family setting up the new enterprise, gave us a tour. I felt that I had walked into the pages of Tom Brown's Schooldays. The uppermost floors remained untouched since its 19th century days as a boarding school; the mahogany-walled, open-topped sleeping stalls for the pupils were still in situ. How stark and unwelcoming the small cubicles looked and I thought of the many new boys who must have suffered the pangs of home-sickness there, as well as terror at the thought of the phantom housemaid! The legend of the haunting persisted to the end of the 20th century, when the tale was retold by my daughter to discourage the midnight corridor wanderings of her students. After my visit I reported back to my colleagues in Italy. I felt the set-up at Hurst Court as both living and teaching accommodation held great promise. My next job was to advertise for host families. The response to the advert was tremendous. Although it specified that the host families should live reasonably close to Hurst Court, the good accommodation rate we offered attracted responses from all over the town. After a week of running to the telephone day and night I had compiled a list of possible families and homes to inspect. I felt it was a privilege to be allowed into peoples' homes and thought back to my own days of being vetted as a hostess and wondered how, 30 years previously, my home and I had measured up. I did not expect to see every corner of the house, just those rooms that would be used by the student - their bedroom, the bathroom, the living room and, of course, the kitchen. Time was also spent talking to the hostess and her husband, if he was at home. I saw a wide variety of homes: Some were like show houses, with fresh décor, well polished furniture and every convenience, others humble and sadly shabby.

One hostess offered a complete granny annex, with its own bathroom, sitting room and two bedrooms. One of these contained a lace-pillow-heaped, double bed, which fitted into a romantic arched alcove; the hostess was a superb cook. This house and host family were the closest to those that used be portrayed on the languages schools' publicity brochures for the foreign families – picture perfect.

In another house two children squabbled over a mean snack while I was shown the accommodation on offer for a pair of students. It was a small, single bedroom, furnished with just one tiny chest of drawers and two 30 inches-wide folding beds, with mattresses as thin as a sliced-bread sandwich. When I murmured that the room was not quite what I was looking for the hostess bridled, saying, 'But I have had students from (naming a famous organisation) for years!' One neglected and rambling Victorian house I inspected was home to eleven students at the height of the season. The hostess was in full-time employment and the students were looked after by an au pair who had little command of English. I was shown all over the house, at one point squeezing past a grubby Stannah stair-lift fixed to the wall of a flight of rickety stairs. I bet the students had a heck of a time on that thing! I thought about fire precautions and when does a home stop being a host family and become a hostel. I think it's when the number of guests exceeds six.

Another vetting-visit was to a beautiful modern home that had a big farmhouse-style kitchen and two spare double bedrooms. When our two students were placed there, one girl kept running every morning to her friend, boarded with a nearby family, to use their toilet. I discovered that the hostess with the two double rooms had replaced the four single beds with six bunk beds and was homing 12 students. However, our student refused the offer to be re-homed; she was happy in the 'hostel', the hostess was likeable, the food good and the company wonderful. The student did not care that she, we and several other language organisations had been hoodwinked. I inspected a bungalow on the Ridge, next door but one to Lavender Cottage, the former home of the late Emilie Crane, the lady who inspired the start of my writing career some few years later. My main concern about the bungalow, a lovely property inside and out, with a charming family in residence, was that it was home to a huge dog, a blue Great Dane, a wonderfully soppy creature – but some students are terrified of dogs.

Generally, homes fell somewhere in the middle of the range, they were clean and comfortable but not over-luxurious. As important as the home, in fact, more so, was the hostess. As each answered my questions about ages and size of her family, domestic pets, if she worked outside the home, what her husband's employment was the family hobbies and interests, she also gave clues whether was the kind of host mother we were looking for. Some said the magic words, 'When the students are here I look upon them as my own children and I treat them the way I would want my children to be treated if they were living with a family in another country.' And they did just that. The host families of Hastings and St Leonards are the backbone of the overseas student business and have been for decades. I cannot say enough good things about the majority of those I met.

As my first season of working for the organisation got underway I was asked to book the ferry crossings, coach excursions, visits to Hastings attractions, sports activities and to advertise for local teachers of English. My daughter and her colleague made a short visit to Hastings in April to carry out the interviews for teachers of English as a foreign language, (EFL) as well as to have their first look at Hurst Court, which was by then beginning to shape up very well. The prospective EFL teachers were attracted by the rate of pay but not by the short duration of the courses. Some took the post, only to let us down at the last minute. At the time we had no understanding of that employment market and were outraged! My colleagues decided to broaden the school's curriculum, so I was instructed to advertise for teachers of drama, art, photography, archery and fishing. The applicants for that post reached 60 and then I stopped counting.

By early July we had over 100 students boarded in the locality, some at Broomham Hall and others at Hurst Court and about 30 in host families, mostly in Ore Village and along the eastern end of the Ridge. For this trip my colleagues in Italy had hired two coaches, a single and a double-decker, from Signor Persigilli of Milan. In addition to bringing the students to the UK, these luxurious, air-conditioned vehicles were used as taxis to transport the students hither and thither, always accompanied by my daughter or her colleague, who carefully handed them out of the left-hand drive coach, lest they should step into the traffic. While other students jostled for taxis or waited for late night buses, our students rode home in state, each one delivered in the coach to the host family's front door. At a student welfare meeting I overheard my colleagues and I described by another language school owner as 'housewives just playing at it.' To a degree, he was right but in Milan parents were queuing up to send their children to Hastings with our 'mother hen' organisation.

For the first week of the students' residence in Hurst Court in 1995 I slept there, sharing my daughter's double bedroom. It was very comfortable - south facing and airy, with a new hand basin, coffee making facilities, fitted carpets, good beds with soft duvets and bouncy mattresses. However, once again the food was a problem. I think that Italians must be the most fastidious eaters in Europe. Complaints were made and the cook was understandably offended; the meals at Hurst Court were imaginative and well cooked but it was this pasta thing again. So from the luggage lockers in the coaches my daughter brought forth catering-sized quantities of Italian olive oil, pasta and hefty bricks of parmesan cheese. The cook submitted to directions about pasta being cooked 'al dente' and a measure of harmony on the question of food was reached.

Broomham was kept for the younger students on the trip; its rural location provided the security and simpler recreations more suitable for the younger teens. It is my opinion that a language-study trip is wasted on younger children but I thought the boarding school environment made all the difference. The ratio of chaperones to children was high, they had plenty of friends with them and they did not have to cope with the stresses of family and daily life in a foreign country or speak English for most of the time but in all honesty as far as it being a cultural experience goes, they could have been anywhere. I was often invited to go on the coach trips the students took but I limited my excursions with them to short, evening outings. Stereotypically, Italians are very noisy people, so are teenagers everywhere and the prospect of being shut in a coach with them all day was not attractive. Besides, I was more useful at "base camp", to deal with emergencies. The host families, learning about my ready availability, kept me busy with daily queries or complaints. The students did not seem to realise that they had come to live in a closely-knit community, where host families were often related. A grouse from one student to another about their host family was innocently passed to the relative of the offending household; the problem was fleas. The flea-host was the family's cat but it was ruffled feathers I had to smooth!

The Italian parents became confused by the locations at which their children were boarded and not getting a reply from the public telephone in the reception hall of the schools, they telephoned my home number, any hour of the day and night. So I put together my own litany of explanations in simple Italian. Although I could speak the language to a modest level I could not understand it well. I had practically no experience of Italian conversation, so I coped with this by talking non-stop, with my various prepared statements; "They are in London today. The coach is late home because there is much traffic on the motorway. The correct number of their school is…Your child is safe and well. Ring me again later if you are still worried." (This was a killer suggestion from me – they did, repeatedly. My Italian improved no end!) I kept my sanity by thinking; "If it was my child…" The several years that I had worked on a telephone helpline for the desperate stood me in good stead.

At the end of the visit, the Italian students who had taken the drama classes gave a presentation to the Hastings Mayor, their host families, fellow students and all the teachers in the assembly hall of Hurst Court. Considering some of the children were very young and had almost no English and the teachers spoke no Italian the production was very successful. I defy anyone not to be moved by the sound of children singing. (Even though one item was the toe-curling 'My Heart Will Go On' from the film "Titanic!") In August my daughter returned to Hastings for a personal visit with her husband and children, to escape the exhausting humidity of Milan. She was greeted by the news that the management of Broomham Hall would not be able to offer student accommodation for the next year, the year in which the new business partner hoped to bring even more students. As my daughter was in Hastings for three weeks she decided to try and find another residence that could accommodate groups. I had heard mention during that summer of a very large house, called Caple-ne-Ferne, used for student accommodation. I booked an appointment for a visit to the house and to meet the management. The word 'house' seemed a misnomer; the place was a mansion, with a turret and half-timbering but it was not as old as Hurst Court and many centuries younger than Broomham. I knew nothing then of the building's origins but several years later I put together a potted history.

'Caple-ne-Ferne is a Victorian mansion, designed by architects Jeffery and Skiller in 1897. It has had varied uses since its construction as a family home. Major and Mrs Tubbs were its first occupants; Mrs Tubbs had female friends who were active in the nascent Hastings Women's Movement and it is believed that famous local supporters of women's liberation, such as Doctor Elizabeth Blackwell and Doctor Sophia Jex Blake, would meet at Caple-ne-Ferne, to discuss political tactics over tea. By 1892, Mrs Tubbs was a widow but she continued to live alone in the mansion until her death. In 1922 the house was bought by the London and General Omnibus Company and it opened as a convalescent home in 1923. Such was the

popularity of Caple-ne-Ferne, that in 1927 an 86-bed extension was added. The house subsequently became the convalescent home for the Transport and General Workers Union and in 1956 an adjoining building was acquired. The administrators of the concern had strong communist sympathies and the convalescent home earned a local reputation for being a hotbed of 'lefty goings on'. A very famous visitor to Caple-ne-Ferne in the 1960s was Russia's President Brehznev.'

My husband saw a cavalcade of black cars passing through Ore Village late one night in the 60s, as he walked our Labradors and he wondered who it was that needed so many motor cycle outriders. Now we know!

Immediately after inspecting Caple-ne-Ferne and coming to an informal agreement with owner Dan Tranter and his business partner that we would use his accommodation the next year, we heard that the Broomham School management had changed their plans and the building would be available to us in 1996. Now we had an embarrassment of accommodation. My daughter returned to Hastings in September with her business partner to finalise plans with Mr Tranter and to promote an idea they had conceived; a student exchange between the local, day-pupils of Broomham and those of a school in the suburbs of Milan. My daughter gave an inspiring presentation to the parents of the Broomham children, describing the scheme, set for the spring, in which the Italian school children would stay with the families of Broomham children and in return the Italian parents would give accommodation to the English children.

My daughter decided to hold a party in Milan in October 1995 for the Italian students who had visited Hastings that summer. The event was an opportunity to present the certificates that the students had attained during the summer and to promote the next year's courses. I decided to go the party. It was not a good flight; the plane stood for three hours on the runway at Gatwick after we had boarded; 'fog in Milan' causing the delayed take-off. For most of the flight visibility was poor, the clouds breaking only as we approached Milan, giving flashes of rice fields far below, as they reflected the evening sunshine. My daughter met me at the airport with a red rosebud, a typically Italian gesture. On reaching her apartment I was immediately plunged into the hectic pattern of my daughter's life; we hurtled about in her little car from one appointment another; to the printer to pick up publicity leaflets, to check the arrangements at the party venue and, for some obscure reason, to a gymnasium. We called at the homes of various students and afterwards we sat on a committee meeting at a school, chaired by a priest. Wine was served throughout the discussions, the priest consuming more than anybody. Whether any satisfactory agreement was met was beyond me, as the Italian was spoken at such a rate as to be unintelligible but the meeting broke up with much kissing, which I interpreted as a good sign.

Next day my son-in-law, my two teenage granddaughters and I devoted hours to the preparations for the forthcoming event; each student's certificate was carefully rolled and tied with red silk ribbon, music was selected, balloons inflated and the food prepared. At last I understood why our sandwiches are so appalling to Italians. The students' party sandwiches were superb. They were made with a variety of bread rolls and flat-breads, some baked with black or green olives and others with herbs and olive oil, all sufficiently tasty to be eaten alone. But they were filled with generous slices of delicious hams, salamis and different cheeses. Now, that's what you call a sandwich! A celebration cake, to provide 200 portions, was collected from the baker, where I found that my daughter was well known, as indeed she was in the whole community, thanks to her reputation as a teacher. I should mention that during party preparations, B's students appeared at intervals for lessons and on one occasion I was roped in to make English conversation with a more advanced pupil. The presentation event was planned to take place over two days, one party on Saturday evening and the other on Sunday afternoon, in an attempt to accommodate guests who might be held back by the notorious Milanese fog. Both parties were a success and I was very interested to meet the students' parents. Face-to-face, my inadequate Italian seemed to be understood, albeit augmented by smiles and conventional niceties, or perhaps it was getting better? During the Sunday afternoon the party was interrupted by the news that my son-in-law's brother had just become a father. This called for an immediate trip to the region where I had attended the new parents' wedding. Everything at the Italian hospital was just that bit different from our own, giving me the feeling that I had slipped into a parallel universe. But the happiness that a new baby brings to a family is universal and a lovely thing to observe, even if the big baby boy was curious purple-reddish shade, due to a difficult delivery. I understand he's a very handsome child now.

My trip home was beautiful, with perfect visibility all the way. The uninterrupted view of Europe sliding away beneath me was the clearest I had ever seen. Glaciers in the Alps gleamed like sheets of molten steel and after this there were hundreds of miles of red and brown arable land, now autumn naked, interspersed with small farming communities, looking vulnerable from the sky. In sombre mood I pondered that this was the view seen by WWII bombers as they passed overhead bearing death and destruction.

The April 1996 Broomham exchange trip was not an unmitigated success. The coach driver who drove the children to England with a view to remaining for the duration of the trip, mysteriously disappeared shortly after arrival. Rumours circulated that he was escaping a failed love affair or an irate husband - perhaps both, we never discovered. The owner of the coach business flew to England to take over the assignment. As back-up transport for the children's excursions, Dan Tranter got hold of a semi-retired Empress Coach which he said he would drive. The coach was painted bright pink and was instantly named the Barbie-Bus. There were not enough Broomham families to accommodate the Italian children so other host families had to be found, one taking in a group of four children and two teachers from Italy, who were not pleased with this arrangement. There was also an incident with minor hostility towards the students by local teenagers. This and other matters lead to endless complaints from the teachers and the children. And the weather was terrible. I understand that the reverse exchange trip was also not very successful. It was a venture we did not repeat.

As far as my preparation for the Italian students' courses were concerned the spring of 1996 was the same routine as in the previous year except that with the higher numbers expected, the accommodation sources had to be increased and the number of teachers required would be greater. I always found interviewing EFL teachers very stressful and I think my daughter did too; we were as nervous as the applicants. Their personal qualities were as important as their qualifications - it had to be remembered that this was partly a holiday scheme and a certain lightness of touch was required. I recall one applicant; a middle-aged man who had been teaching EFL for years. He had a scruffy appearance and an off-hand approach to the interview that lost him the job. At a subsequent round of interviews he applied again and as we were by then desperate, we took him on. The students loved him, his laid-back style and years of EFL teaching experience made him ideal for the job and the students learned well in his class. So much for our judgment!

Just before the arrival of the summer 1996 students, when I hoped that most of my preparations for their trip were finished, I took a part-time job, minding an antique shop three and a half days a week. It was a strange kind of work, much of it just sitting and waiting. I did do quite a bit of dusting and vacuuming, with fits of rearranging stock, adding my own touches of fresh flowers and aromatherapy oil lamps; making a home from home in fact. I also read lots of books. It's almost a tradition that such shops become a drop-in centre for people who want to idle some time away and just talk. They hardly ever buy anything and the hapless shop-sitter becomes the receptacle for the world's woes. The shop work was in no way a refuge from the inevitable problems and stresses associated with the students and I was on constant call, but not as much as my colleagues, who had no time off at all.

Some of our Italian youngsters fell victim to the anti-student violence that was endemic in Hastings and St Leonards; a common problem in many south east coastal towns. The term violence is something of a catch-all, as much of the behaviour never exceeded the level of playground bullying but it was still frightening, even if it was only jeers and unfulfilled threats. At that time police statistics showed that the average age of the perpetrators of this crime was 14 to 16 years and the victims were of the same age. Sometimes injuries did occur and it was my daughter's misfortune to be a victim. A gang of teenage boys chased her and a group of her younger students down London Road, in St Leonards. Trying to evade them, my daughter shepherded her students onto the seafront but the boys ran through Norman Road and accosted them at the seaward end of Warrior Square. The local boys had broken bottles in their hands, which they threw at the students. One bottle caught my daughter's calf a glancing blow, making a small cut. The police were called but by the time they arrived the boys had run off. After taking a brief statement from my daughter the police drove her around to try to spot her assailant, who had red hair. She saw him sitting on a seat in Warrior Square with the other culprits and was astonished that the police did not make an arrest or at least question him but it seems that British police procedure is not the same as that in Italy. Further police investigations were carried out but the students' departure was imminent and so the case never came to court. The cunning young assailants were aware that they had near-immunity from police prosecution because of the expense and complications of bringing witnesses back from other countries, a situation which was to eventually change.

On one occasion I was caught up in an attack on a group of overseas students. In the spring of 1999 my colleagues brought several groups of 14 and 15-year-old students to Hastings during term time, a rare concession by the Italian education authorities. They came by air and there was no private coach this time. These groups tended to be from the same school; often the students were in the same class. They were placed with host families as near to each other as possible, for security and convenience. The first group of students arrived from Italy quite late in the afternoon and they and the host families were told that the youngsters were forbidden go out that evening, as they had an early start for English lessons in the morning. We had reckoned without the scheming adolescents. They colluded on lies to be told to the host families, namely that a surprise event had been organised and the students had to go out at 8.00pm, to meet at the bus stop outside the supermarket in Ore Village, their previously arranged assembly point for the next morning's journey to lessons. This paved area, with its public seat, is the nearest thing Ore has to a village green and is a traditional gathering place for young people.

When a crowd of some 30 noisy foreigners converged on the territory of the local boys they started throwing punches. Some of the bigger male students stood their ground to protect the girls, but generally speaking, Italians are not belligerent. The degree of seriousness of the confrontation was never defined but it was enough to send some of the students running and crying into the maze of surrounding streets. A few quickly made it back to their host families and relayed dramatised reports of the event. Some phoned their own families in Italy with exaggerated stories and panic ensued. My colleagues and I were immediately informed and a search party was organised by host fathers in cars, to track down the lost students. All were given a good telling-off and the experience seemed enough to render them obedient. We informed the police of the incident but although it was distressing for us, it was rather small stuff for an overstretched police force. They did provide a police officer one evening, to watch the bus stop; of course, there was no trouble that time.

However, in the long term the police could only give advice, not ongoing support. But it was not the end of the matter. The local yobs had found a new sport. They quickly learned the routine of the students and began harassing them when they got off the local bus at teatime, returning from their lessons. For their evening excursions the students had to meet at the village bus stop and again they were sitting targets. My daughter and I, both small and not particularly threatening women, acted as escorts. One evening, a crowd of about 10 local boys and, to their shame, some girls, had gathered at the supermarket bus stop for the evening's fun, jeering and shouting. My daughter, all four foot eleven of her, was enraged and confronted one boy. He was aged about 12, plump and pink; he looked like a choir boy. She said to him; "Why do you do this? These students are just children like you, they are not rich. Their parents have made sacrifices to send their children here. Would you like it if you were bullied if you went to Italy?" He meekly shook his head. The bus arrived and the frightened students surged towards its open door, with my daughter and I squashed among them. The local youngsters ran up the flight of steps at the side of the supermarket and onto its flat roof which overlooked the bus stop. They began to spit at us and throw down drink cans that contained dregs of sweet, sticky liquid, which splattered our clothing. I looked up and saw among the mob the 'choir boy', yelling with ugly glee. Eventually, the students became philosophical about the incident and said they had witnessed or suffered similar or worse treatment from teenagers in Italy.

Ten days after the first attack I got a phone call from a senior police officer. He questioned me about the original incident and I explained that it was the deception by the students of their host families that had triggered the pattern of hostile behaviour. However, someone had to be blamed and as I was the only person available that represented the school, it was me. I was given an old fashioned dressing-down and told that the students should not have been let out.

Some time after I had retired from the overseas student organisation I was talking to a group of men in their middle thirties. One of them admitted to harassing students in his teens. He said, 'Me and my mates used to go into the amusements arcades when we were about 15 and the foreign students would come in, taking up our space and jabbering in their language, we knew they were laughing about us. We used to kick the students' bags about when they put them on the floor and sometimes there would be fights. It was daft really because my mum had students at home and I got on with them OK.' Other local lads, particularly the motor cyclists, my own son among them, had student contact of a more amicable sort in mind. They would gather at the entrance to Hastings Pier to admire and chat up the enchanting foreign girls at the student discos.

For over 30 years Hastings Pier ballroom was THE nightspot for underage foreign students. Alcohol-free discos were organised on the pier for youngsters of all the local language schools; they attended in their hundreds, numbers only limited by the health and safely regulations. Not only did the venue give them the opportunity to socialise easily with students from other countries if their school was a single-nationality organisation, but the pier also created the unique feeling of being on a kind of cruise liner that never actually went to sea; this seemed to accentuate the romance of the evening. In recent years, a browse round the message boards on Hastings websites finds nostalgic recollections of the pier disco nights enjoyed by former students ten, twenty, thirty years ago. My daughter's students were no exception to the trend. During the mid-1990s there was a particular DJ who had the soft, almost feminine good looks which young girls find non-threatening and therefore appealing. He was that year's idol for the Italian girls. Two were so smitten that on hearing it was his birthday that day they forwent their supper at the host family and begged the mother to help them bake and ice a chocolate cake to present to him. It is a mark of the kindliness of this lady that she agreed. When my daughter had her autumn end-of-season party in Milan for her students, the girls wanted the Hastings Pier DJ to play the music for their party. He went on an all-expenses-paid trip to Italy and was feted socially. The innocent girls were totally unaware that while they were sighing over the golden good looks of their hero he was quietly doing the same over the dark-eyed, dark-haired Italian boys.

My two half-Italian granddaughters and their parents had visited Hastings each summer for some years before my daughter began her student trips. The girls were bilingual from an early age and after a few annual visits they were sufficiently confident of their English and their whereabouts to go out alone. Their fluent English and grasp of the culture protected them from the violence that overseas students suffered and they sometimes stepped in when they found one of their compatriots lost or frightened. The crime against students as we know it now was not so prevalent then. When my granddaughters reached young adulthood they were able to take on the role of leaders to groups of their mother's students and escort them on excursions. On one such outing, my elder granddaughter, then aged about 18, was supervising a walk over Hastings' eastern cliff-top wildlife reserve with a class of younger children. They were approached and threatened by a group of about six teenage boys, one of whom was armed with a spade. My granddaughter told her charges to run away, while she faced up to the boys alone; madness in my opinion, as they could have been on drugs. But the yobs were taken aback by her perfect English and they cleared off, realizing that they had threatened somebody who might be a local and would be able to act as an articulate witness in court.

With so much emphasis on local youngsters who behave badly towards the students it can easily be overlooked that the overseas students sometimes get out of hand. The saddest of these is the reluctant student. Some parents sent their children on the courses because they believed it would be a useful experience, regardless of their child's wishes. Worse still, these parents often refused the option of placing the child in the boarding school accommodation where they would at least have had the support of their friends but instead they chose host family residence. The child, sometimes as young as 13 and not speaking English well, had to face struggles with the language every day. This sometimes resulted in refusal to eat, tears, social withdrawal, even bed-wetting. This unhappy situation seemed to bring out the best in host families but it was very hard work.

Much worse are the brats. In summer 1999 we had a group of students, all from the same school – a private establishment for the children of the wealthy, children who had in some cases been excluded from state schools because of their conduct. One of these was a tall, powerfully built 15-year old-boy, who came unwillingly on the three-week course, at the instruction of his father. The boy was trouble from the start, smoking, swearing and being physically aggressive to the girl students. He was removed from his host family to live in the boarding school where he could be more closely supervised. But he destroyed school property and tried to set fire to a girl's hair while on the school coach. He was booked on an early return flight but his father said that if his son was sent home prematurely he would immediately send him back to England. There are brat parents too, it seems. However, a sudden, 'mystery illness' prevented the boy's return home until the group's appointed departure day.

For three weeks one summer we accommodated a group of students in Catsfield Place, which was also used by Broomham School for boarding and teaching accommodation. It is in a remote spot between the villages of Catsfield and Crowhurst and approached by a narrow lane and driveway that hardly gave passage to the huge Italian coach. Catsfield Place, like Broomham is part of the Ashburnham family estate and is a mellow-stone, part tile-hung Grade II listed country house, dating from the 16th century, which was altered and enlarged in the 17th and 18th century. Some of the original interior oak panelling still exists, as does a heavy oak staircase dating from 1685. My daughter stayed there with the students and she was thrilled to be in such a historic house. One night, during the students' occupancy, there was a thunderstorm; the flashes of lightning gleamed on the shields and swords suspended above a great inglenook fireplace and there was much screaming when a girl swore she saw a ghost and had hysterics. How they all enjoyed the fuss! However, totally oblivious of the unique opportunity they had in living surrounded by history, the students complained; they hated the Spartan household arrangements, once again the food was heavily criticized and they said that the outdoor swimming pool was too cold to use and there was nothing to do. There must have been some children who enjoyed the location but these were probably the quiet ones, whose opinions went unheard. I would love to hear their now thirty-something views of Catsfield Place. This ten bedroom country house with over 3 acres of land is now on the market for over one and a quarter million pounds.

My colleagues in Italy, who had returned to Hastings so many times with the same students, thought that different locations for the trips should be found. To break new ground they proposed to take students to stay in London and one other place; after some discussion we settled on Southampton as a second destination. In October 1997 we spent 36 hours in Southampton, looking for a residence and a source of teachers. As it is a university city, teachers would be easy to find and we were offered accommodation and teaching rooms for our students at the nearby Warsash Maritime Centre, a training school for the Merchant Navy. I was impressed by the sleeping, eating, studying and sports arrangements at the centre, everything so clean and 'ship shape'. The buildings were in an open, breezy location, with neat gardens and lawns that swept down to a yacht launch. By the time the students arrived in July 1998 everything was ready in Southampton; teachers hired, menus agreed and a programme of new and interesting activities and excursions prepared. What we had not prepared for was the culture clash between the Maritime Centre staff and the rowdy, adolescent Italians, who in no way resembled the usual disciplined and responsible occupants of the building. It was exacerbated by the students being in the charge of the Italian headmistress, who though efficient in organising things on paper was hopeless at discipline. Making this problem worse was the fact that some Italian teachers seem to go in fear of upsetting parents and, as one told me, 'The Italian birthrate is very low, families often have only one child, who is made to believe they are a little emperor.'

I mentioned earlier in this book that our students were destined to to stay in a real castle with a moat - this was Herstmonceux Castle in Sussex. I had been aware of the existence of the building for years but only as a place seen in a valley, on the way to visit relatives living at Hailsham. Years ago, before the trees grew so tall, it was still possible to see the turrets of the castle and the domes of its observatory from the main road. My young children wondered how to prounounce the signpost and decided it was Herstmonsocks.

My colleagues and I were very interested to learn that during the summer vacations the owners of the castle hired out the building and all its facilites to overseas students. We went to view Herstmonceux Castle as potential student accommodation in late September 1998. It was one of those sweltering days when summer lingers and our first close view of the castle was seeing its red brick image mirrored in the moat, which is actually a lake. The castle has turrets and towers; the two highest are 84 feet and stand at the gatehouse, approached via a drawbridge. No wonder it was chosen in 1989, by the BBC, to film sequences for an adaptation of one of the Narnia books, "The Silver Chair". On entering the long, sloping drive that runs down to the hollow in which the castle sits, you pass an observatory with several metal domes, a curious contrast with the ancient building beyond. The present castle is not quite as ancient as romanticism led me to believe, as its website tells:

'The first written evidence of existence of the Herste settlement appears in William the Conqueror's Domesday Book, which reports that one of William's closest supporters granted tenancy of the manor at Herste to a man named Wilbert. By the end of the 12th century the family at the manor house at Herste had considerable status. Written accounts mention a lady called Idonea de Herste who married a Norman nobleman called Ingelram de Monceux, a name that eventually became Herstmonceux. A descendent of the Monceux line, Sir Roger Fiennes, was ultimately responsible for the construction of Herstmonceux Castle. He was appointed Treasurer of the Household to Henry VI. Fiennes needed a house fitting his position and so construction of the castle began in 1441; his position as treasurer made it possible for him to afford the £3,800 building costs. Eventually, the castle fell into ruin and was demolished in 1777 and a Flemish brick castle was erected on the site. It was an unusual material for its time and is today the oldest significant brick building still standing in England. The builders of Herstmonceux Castle concentrated more on grandeur and comfort than on defence but it presents a breathtaking site, set in 500 acres of park and woodland.

The property passed through a number of private owners until it was sold in 1946 to the Admiralty. In 1957 the castle grounds became home to the Royal Greenwich Observatory and remained so until 1988, when it was moved to Cambridge. Several of the telescopes are still on the Herstmonceux site. In 1992, Alfred Bader, a refugee from Nazi Germany, who made his home in Canada, learned of the castle's vacancy and offered to buy the estate for his wife, who declined the gift, saying that there were too many rooms to clean. Bader, an alumnus of Queens University, Kingston Ontario, asked if he could donate the castle to the university as an international study centre. The castle was extensively renovated and began its new life in 1994.'

Not that the history of the castle would interest the Italian students of the age we were planning for, mainly aged 13 to 16. The students' rooms were very comfortable; each double bedroom was well furnished and had a wash basin with bathrooms close by. There was a fully equipped gymnasium and sports pitches and hundreds of surrounding acres of lovely woodland, teeming with wildlife. (We hired an expert in local flora and fauna to give talks and to supervise walks and woodcraft instruction to our students.) The university meals were served in the castle cafeteria, a good selection of hot and cold dishes and desserts; the salads looked delicious. Some of our students took their lessons in the castle. What a setting for studies! I never got a chance to sleep or dine at Herstmonceux, something I would have like to have done very much. It was not easy to find EFL teachers to go that far out of town to work, so the inducement of travel expenses and free lunch were added to the package. Even then some teachers dropped out. I think this may have been partly due to the behaviour of the students, who were aware that the Italian headmistress, who supposedly had overall control, had nothing of the kind. At one point she was admonished by the castle staff for her indifference to the wild behaviour of the male students. I organised a Hastings football team to play against the Italian boys on the castle pitch. It was a scruffy game; the Italian boys were rude and badly behaved, spitting and swearing, exploiting the fact that they were younger and smaller than the English boys, who for this reason let them get away with it. The Hastings team decided there would be no more such contests. A pity, as football games played by these local lads against other Italians and a French team had been very sporting.

An almost total eclipse the sun occurred on 11th August 1999 and I was touched that my younger granddaughter, who was working as a group leader at Herstmonceux, left the unique opportunity of seeing the eclipse at the castle observatory, to watch it with me in my Ore Village garden. It was also a chance to give her some grandma-style TLC; the girl was exhausted by the long days of duty with no time off, as was her older sister who was working under the same conditions at Hurst Court in Hastings.

During 1999 I had to accept that I had come to the end of my tether and of my multi-faceted work for the students. My home, enhanced by a newly installed Internet connection, had become an office for all who needed one, a sick-bay for ailing students and an 18-hour clearing house for every problem associated with the students. The original idea of the student trips had grown into something monstrous. They were never intended to be a commercial enterprise, just a jolly way to bring my daughter, her family and some students on a summer holiday to Hastings. I was sad at giving up; in spite of the stress there had been a lot of satisfaction and fun in the work. I had enjoyed the feeling of being useful and I had come to know many decent and friendly families in my community, via the school's accommodation work. I quite liked being known as " the student lady."

The student visits organised by my daughter and her colleague continued for the next few years but with diminishing numbers. A scheme of accommodating students with hosts who were also teachers was launched. The students staying under this arrangement were boarded close to each other and this allowed them to undertake a kind of musical chairs tuition round, swapping homes and teachers by the hours.

On July 7th 2005 my granddaughters were in transit from Italy, via London. Although we knew the girls were in no immediate danger, the terrorist attack on the Underground seemed to mark a watershed for my daughter, whose health was not good and she decided to end the student trips to Hastings. With this cessation went my last contact with the present-day business of overseas students, founded on the hospitality and kindness of Hastings families.

My eldest granddaughter at age 17 met her husband-to-be when as students they both travelled on the coach across Europe on one of her mother's annual school trips to Hastings. Their friendship grew over the following ten years and they were married in Milan in June 2006, forty-two years after I had taken the life-changing step of responding to the newspaper advert that said, "Host Families Wanted."

CHAPTER THREE

STUDENTS IN UNIFORM

On August 12th 1939, a group of French students who had made their first visit to Hastings the previous year, posed for a newspaper photograph at Hastings Grammar School. They numbered about one hundred; mature looking girls and boys, portrayed in the company of their tutor Monsieur Forget and Grammar School head, Mr Hyder and French Teacher, Mr Miller. To celebrate the second anniversary of their visit they decided to adopt the title, Anglo- French Holiday School. With the threat of war looming, the students were forced to make a premature departure from Hastings on 26th August. These visits were not a one-way arrangement: Under the auspices of the Grammar School's senior French master the school had made trips to St Malo in 1933, Paris in 1934, 1938 and 1939, Belgium in 1935 and 1936 and Germany in 1937. The trips were not revived after WWII but some of the sixth-form German language students attended an international summer-course in the mid-sixties at Gottingen, near Hanover in what was then West Germany. The Iron Curtain, with its electrified fences, minefields and watchtowers ran across the hills and farmland only a few kilometres to the east of the town. It was an unforgettable sight but possibly conveyed a more ambiguous message than the course organizers could have wished.

With the outbreak of war, student trips to Hastings and St Leonards ceased but not the arrival of overseas visitors. Hundreds of young men came to the area with the military, some recruits younger than the carefree students we see today. But these wartime 'students' had come to Hastings to learn the language of conflict and destruction.

In the 1940s, Hastings was rather insular in its attitudes; even visitors from neighbouring towns were regarded as foreigners. The influx of battalions of soldiers from the UK and overseas into a sleepy seaside town was a something of a culture shock. The earliest arrivals were a few Norwegians, who had accompanied our own troops when they evacuated Norway to escape the invading Germans. The Norwegians wanted to continue the fight and being expert mountaineers they joined the newly formed Commandos and trained on the Hastings cliffs. By far the greatest number of new arrivals came with the Canadian Military, most of whom were billeted in large, empty hotels and big houses and abandoned boarding schools in and around the town, some of which were used in the 1990s to house overseas students. For example: Hurst Court and Broomham Hall.

Some of the soldiers were billeted with families; one of these was 18 year old Canadian Doug Powell who lodged with a family in Lower Broomgrove. Nearby lived the Brewer family and their daughter Joyce.

Joyce said:
'My family soon made friends with the all the Canadians, but most particularly with Doug, who was from Nova Scotia. Doug resembled the famous film star Roy Rogers and like him, he had a pleasant singing voice. Mum made him and all the soldiers welcome; she used to sew on their battledress stripes and flashes, darn their socks and give them meals from the family's meagre rations. Dad used to let the soldiers come into the house for a game of billiards, on a quarter-sized billiard table, which also served as an indoor refuge during air raids, until our Morrison Shelter was delivered.'

It was noticeable how big most of the Canadians were in comparison with British youths, who had been brought up during the depression. During these years the poor in Britain suffered badly from inadequate nutrition and lack of medical and dental treatment and so our boys looked weedy in comparison with their Canadian cousins. Many Hastings families emigrated to Canada in the early 20th century and their sons returned to fight for their mother country in both World Wars.

There were Americans stationed in the area, who would pay visits to Hastings. A wartime teen-age boy, Noel Care, recalls the American visitors:

'They seemed bewildered, not at all like the Canadian soldiers, who seemed to feel at home right from the start. From the way they spoke it

seems the Americans had not long left home but they all sported the Service Overseas Medal, which they received after their initial training. Their officers must have forgotten to include the realities of war in training because when the siren sounded in Hastings the American soldiers looked anxiously for an air raid shelter, while locals just carried on regardless.'

By 1943 the Queens Hotel and the adjoining Albany Hotel had been taken over by the military for accommodation; the Albany was home to the Royal Canadian Hussars. On Sunday 23rd May a bomb entered a window of the Queens Hotel, slid along a table, exited through a wall and hit the Albany Hotel. Fortunately, because it was Sunday, most of the soldiers were out of the buildings. When the rescue services reached the Albany they found that the uninjured Canadians were trying to carry out rescue work themselves, but they had no experience of dealing with demolished buildings. Many of them were suffering from severe cuts to hands and arms, sustained during their frantic efforts. The work to clear the site of the ruined Albany Hotel went on for several days. Since I recorded this incident in my book Letters to Hannah I have heard from a Canadian reader, Allan Notman, who as a young WWII soldier stationed in Hastings, was one of the lucky ones not in the Albany when the bomb hit.

In a letter dated 24th May 1943 headed, 'under an improvised tent in a field' and addressed to his sweetheart, Maisie, Alan wrote:

'Well I have certainly seen life since I last wrote. Yesterday morning everything was peaceful when at 1.15 the banshee howled. As it was a general occurrence where we were billeted no one took any notice. I was standing right beside an ack-ack gun on the seafront and saw one of the crew point to some planes on the horizon and the gun swung down, in that direction. Then it happened. I got a glimpse of a lot of planes with black crosses on the wings before I bit the dust. They emptied their machine guns and dropped their 'eggs' then everything was quiet again. I came out from behind cover and what an experience I had. I won't go into gruesome detail but it was pretty 'orrible. As you probably know our billets got it. One minute there was a building standing and the next just a heap of debris. A couple of men I know

*very well are dead and many in the hospital. We worked from 2.00pm
to 6.00pm and then we were moved out here. Just our squadron is out
here as they had to keep some men back to dig for those who are
missing.'*

He wrote again next day telling Maisie that three men were still buried
in the hotel ruins and wondering about the others in hospital:

*'The boys are trying to laugh it off but you can see that it has
impressed them.'*

The Canadians left Hastings in mid-1944 and British gun crews took
over the ack-ack gun near Joyce Brewer's home and stayed until the
latter end of 1944. (Both of Joyce's sisters married British soldiers,
who were billeted in their road). Joyce and her sister Hilda sent letters
to Canadian Doug Powell until he was shipped to fight in Italy, when
all correspondence ceased. The family often spoke of him and
wondered if he survived the war. Decades passed and Joyce and her
mum were living alone, still at the Lower Broomgrove address. Mrs
Brewer enjoyed playing bingo at Hastings Pier and one night she heard
a girl with a Canadian accent among the players. Unaware of the
vastness of Canada, Mrs Brewer mentioned Doug Powell and the
Canadian girl, called Joan, asked the name of his home town. Where
she heard it was Springhill, Nova Scotia she was astonished, she knew
the place and Doug's family. Over a year later, on her return to Canada,
Joan traced Doug, who was by then living in Fredericton, New
Brunswick. Mrs Brewer wrote to Doug, who had remained in the army
for 26 years. Many letters were exchanged until Doug died very
suddenly, aged 60. In 1986 his widow, Betty, while on a tour of the UK
made a flying visit to Hastings to meet Mrs Brewer, who died three
weeks later. Joyce still corresponds with Betty.

A retired police officer, who was in the force from the early 1930s,
wrote these memories of the overseas troops in Hastings:

*'In 1940 Canadian troops arrived in Hastings and accommodation
was provided for them in dwelling houses and hotels, particularly in
Eversfield Place and the Marina. A detachment of the Royal Light
Infantry was notably among them and they quickly formed an excellent*

relationship with local residents and the Hastings Borough Police. They were made temporary members of the police recreation club, where they played billiards, snooker, darts, chess and card games.

Some Canadians joined the police swimming club. On 19th August 1942 the RHLI participated in the disastrous raid on Dieppe in which so many lost their lives. They suffered 3,367 dead, wounded, or taken prisoner. Several other units of the Canadian Army were stationed in or near Hastings and became associated with the Home Guard.

In 1943 some United States Army units were stationed in the rural area around Hastings and they came into to town on occasions. They were usually well behaved and friendly, apart from one dangerous incident which occurred in the bar of the York Hotel, (now a shoe shop), in Wellington Place, Hastings. A US soldier became involved in a heated argument with British soldiers and he drew out an automatic pistol from his tunic and fired two rounds into the ceiling. After a struggle he was disarmed and two Provost Men who were called to the scene handed the offender over to the US military authorities to be dealt with, as prescribed by the Visiting Forces Act. The prisoner was detained in cells at Hastings Police Station and shortly afterwards I was instructed to prepare a committee room for a US Courts Martial in Hastings Town Hall, which had been commandeered as police HQ. This court comprised of three officers, with two fully armed soldiers standing behind them and two more armed guards stationed at the court door. The prisoner was charged with disorderly conduct, carrying a concealed weapon and recklessly firing his pistol into the ceiling of the pub. He was sentenced to 12 months in prison.

It became quite common for Canadian and US troops to be invited into the homes of local residents and this was much appreciated by the soldiers. In many cases the sons and daughters of the residents had enlisted in the armed forces and their parents hoped that their children were also being welcomed into the homes of strangers.'

David Judge, formerly from Hastings, now living in Canada said:

'Regarding visiting soldiers and airmen, there must have been a programme set up to arrange home visits by servicemen who were billeted in Hastings and St. Leonards, probably run by the churches. I

can remember having a couple of French Canadian soldiers visit our home several times for tea and hospitality - I remember a pilot (British) I only knew as Mickey - he visited us quite a few times and we had a photo of him in uniform. I think many of the servicemen were billeted in Marine Court. My mother corresponded with Mickey's parents (not sure where they lived) and heard that he was missing in action. I think she had grown very fond of him and his photo stayed on display until she died.'

Because of food rationing it was often a problem to provide meals for the overseas guests so quite frequently unauthorised 'gifts' from military stores arrived in civilian homes, including sweets for the children. Meat rationing, which began on March 11th 1940, was controlled by price, each person getting 1/10d worth (9p) per week per person, with children under six years old having half a ration. Poultry, offal (liver, kidneys, heart, etc) and sausages remained off ration, as were meals at restaurants.

At Christmas time in 1942, American troops gave a party at their camp for the children of a village outside Hastings, using lorries to collect all the children aged between two and sixteen. The youngsters enjoyed entertainment and played American games, ate doughnuts and peanuts and drank coca cola; one soldier had made a huge box of chocolate fudge. The children were given funds for a treat and each went home with an armful of goodies. Communities where troops were stationed set about doing their best to make their wartime visitors welcome. Some were already billeted in family homes and other Hastings residents were encouraged to entertain the servicemen for a meal or an evening round the fire. During the bitterly cold winter months of 1940 almost 1,000 soldiers made visits to private homes in Hastings and St Leonards. These guests came from Great Britain, Australia, Canada, New Zealand and South Africa. The local Women's Voluntary Service, which had recently moved to more prominent premises in Hastings Town Centre, swung into action and after acquiring the use of St Leonard's Parish Mission Hall they worked at turning the bleak room into a club for servicemen. The WVS plea for furniture, soft furnishings, crockery and a piano brought a generous response and the newspaper photographs of the completed clubroom showed a very comfortable looking set-up.

British hospitality to overseas visitors was given as generously as could be managed in the circumstances, as this account by a US soldier reveals:

'The English people treated us with the greatest kindness. They could not do enough for the GI's. One of my buddies had distant relatives in London, and we went to see them and they invited us for dinner. Even though they had strict rationing for all of their food, they wanted to share it with us. The family consisted of a husband, a wife, and two young children. The main course was a rump roast that weighed about two pounds. We each got two small slices of it. We filled up on potatoes and cabbage - their main staples. After the meal, they told us that the roast was the family ration of meat for the month. We offered them cigarettes, but they refused, so we left some without them knowing about it. Cigarettes were a real luxury, and in some ways, they were better than money. In those days almost everyone smoked, especially in England and Europe. There was no black market in England; at least none that I saw. The people took the war very seriously, and they seemed to put the 'war effort', as they called it, before their own needs. They had a very tough time of it for many years, and yet their spirits always seemed to be high.'

In the spring of 1940, thousands of European refugees came to Great Britain and it was the WVS who received, fed and clothed them. The part the WVS played on the home front in WWII cannot be over-estimated and the range of their tasks was enormous: They re-housed people who were bombed out, distributed ration books, provided servicemen of all free nations with social clubs, held dances and community events and helped with the family problems of service personnel on compassionate leave. On May 22nd 1940, a Belgian steam tug arrived at the landing stage of Hastings Pier. It was packed with women, children and elderly men, who were, 'sea-soaked and haggard'. They carried bundles of belongings that they had snatched from their homes in Belgium ten days previously. The mate of the tug said that everything that could float was getting out and as they left the port it was going up in flames. Once again the WVS was on hand to provide comfort and help. For some time before this event individuals or family groups of refugees had been arriving in Hastings. There were sad cases of local suicides of refugees, who either lived in the Hastings area or made the journey to the coast for the sole purpose of killing themselves. Such suicides seemed to increase after Dunkirk, when the threat of the invasion of Britain by the regime that the refugees had fled became very real. One such suicide, in late May 1940, was that of a 58 year old woman of German nationality and Jewish descent, who had come to Britain to escape Nazi oppression. She had secretly kept a supply of morphine tablets and a hypodermic syringe, because she feared her life might become unbearable; the German occupation of France had brought the enemy to within 22 miles, across the channel from Hastings.

Before the war Hastings and St Leonards was home to many respected foreigners who had resided or owned business in the town for years. These were ordered 20 miles inland, to East Grinstead. In September 1939 there were over 71,000 so called enemy aliens registered in Britain. On the outbreak of war, the police arrested a large number of Germans living in Britain. The government feared that some of these people might be Nazi spies, pretending to be refugees. They were interned and held in various camps all over Britain. Like other refugees they eventually appeared before tribunals, which classified them into three different groups. 'A' class aliens were interned, whereas 'B' class aliens were allowed to leave the camps but had certain restrictions placed upon their movements. The majority of refugees were identified as 'C' class aliens and allowed to go free. In Hastings, even the French monks, who occupied the Jesuit College at Ore place on the Ridge, were moved out of the area.

When the war ended in May 1945 people in Britain gradually began to renew the contact they had lost with family and friends in Europe. New friends were made via a system that was eventually called twinning. In 1947 a sports exchange was set up with Dordrecht. This still continues but in the intervening years much more has developed and now Hastings has four European twin towns: Dordrecht (The Netherlands), Béthune (France), Schwerte (Germany) and Oudenaarde (Belgium), with many flourishing contacts in each location. Twinning really took off in the 1960s. Every year, scores of European twin-town guests are welcomed into Hastings and St Leonards families. Competitive swimming exchanges, the first sporting venture, have broadened into other sports; entrants from Hastings twin-towns run in the annual

March Hastings Half-Marathon. There are also cultural exchanges that embrace music, dance and the visual arts.

The idea behind twinning is that towns in different countries build up a special relationship with each other. Individuals, families and organisations take part in exchange visits and as accommodation is arranged on a reciprocal hospitality basis, friendships are soon formed. By offering each other this hospitality, ordinary people can travel abroad fairly cheaply and, above all, get to know another country's way of life in some depth, in a way that mere tourist trips cannot achieve. Participants travel as a group and enjoy a programme of varied, local events. Language is rarely a problem, Europeans often speak English well, or the British visitors have great fun making themselves understood in the language of the host country. A Hastings Borough Council brochure on the subject claims that it supports twinning to an extent that is most unusual in a town of Hastings' size. It is foremost in this enterprise, providing a part-time Twinning Officer who co-ordinates twinning activities and is able to provide modest grant-aid to groups setting up twinning links with like-minded clubs. There are also civic exchanges, with dignitaries of Hastings' twin towns being invited to such events as the town mayor-making ceremony. But the main emphasis of twinning is on ordinary people making friends with their European neighbours.

'Nettie', whose memories of being an overseas student host mother are recorded elsewhere in this book, also mentioned her connections with twinning.

'The interest in twinning faded for a while and was rekindled by Alf Urban and Peter Burton, who arranged a twinning with the George Sands School in Bethune and the Firehills football club in Hastings, of which Alf was the chairman. In this period, Hastings Borough Council were not really involved with twinning and it was quite some years later that a twinning officer was paid for by the council and the scheme was allocated some funding. We still have many friends in Bethune, although Firehills Football Club no longer twin. My son, Christopher, then aged 11, was in the first group that went over to Bethune, to play against their team. When he was 24 he played in another match against the Bethune team, who were visiting Hastings. (1997). A boy

from Bethune who came to us at age 11 became very involved in the twinning when he grew up and is still on the Bethune committee.'

Apart from the lack of sufficient housing in Hastings and St Leonards in the immediate post-war years it was also the continuing food rationing and the following period of austerity that made the possibility of hosting overseas students unlikely. In May 1954, in common with thousands of young brides, I began my married life living in two rented rooms, with shared use of a bathroom. This was in a guest house in Old London Road. Our landlady had boarded a Chinese schoolgirl, Brenda, for some months – a private arrangement with the nearby Sacred Heart Convent. I recall anecdotes about Brenda cooking her national cuisine for the English family, who said that they had blenched at the prospect of her fried lettuce. Some years later Brenda was seen on UK TV, being interviewed in Hong Kong by Alan Whicker, in a programme in his famous series, Whicker's World. By then she was comfortably matron-like in appearance and more than comfortably rich, after marrying a millionaire. She still sees the children of her host family when she visits the UK.

Although the last vestiges of food rationing still remained, those of meat and bacon, I do not recall handing over any coupons for these commodities during the early weeks of my marriage. But this was in Hastings, a place that has always done things in its own way. At midnight on the 4th July 1954, after 14 years, rationing finally came to an end. Members of the London Housewives' Association held a special ceremony in London's Trafalgar Square to mark De-rationing Day. The Minister of Fuel and Power, Geoffrey Lloyd, burned a large replica of a ration book at an open meeting in his constituency. But the Minister of Food, Major Gwilym Lloyd-George, said that he would keep his as a souvenir and praised all those traders and organisations that had co-operated with the rationing system. For the first time since the war began in 1939 London's Smithfield Market opened at midnight instead of 6.00am and did a roaring trade. Butchers predicted meat prices would soar for the next couple of weeks until the effect of supply and demand took over. As newly-weds, we were pretty hard up, so this did not particularly affect us - my modest housekeeping budget did not run to extravagance.

CHAPTER FOUR

LIKE ONE OF THE FAMILY

A few editions of the 1954 Hastings and St Leonards Observer make references to the presence of foreign students in Hastings:

In April:
'Eight sons and daughters of the members of the Rouen Rotary Club stayed with Hastings families.'

In May:
'Large groups of Dutch and German school children visited Hastings and were present at the mayor-making ceremony at the White Rock Pavilion.'

This event has been a favoured opportunity to show off the town's quaint, official functions to foreign visitors for decades. In the early 21st century the ceremony was enlivened by a former town councillor with a personal grudge, who mounted the steps of the theatre's stage and struck the incoming mayor on the face with a glove, shouting, 'You have insulted my wife!' The party of French guests, who are mentioned in the local newspaper as being present, must have been either bemused or enchanted by this archaic gesture, possibly thinking it part of the ceremony.

The White Rock Pavilion was also the scene in a case of overseas student misbehavior in 1954:

'Fifty French students were banned from attending a Humphrey Lyttelton jazz concert held there because of previous noisy behaviour at jazz concerts. Bandleader Ambrose, at an earlier concert, told students to shut up, after they had been whistling, stamping and shouting during the performance. Students were also criticized by young locals for jiving during dances at Hastings Pier, something local youngsters were banned from doing.'

In order to compile this next section of the book I interviewed some of Hastings and St Leonards' many host families. An article requesting memories of hosting overseas students was run in the local newspaper. The response was not encouraging. As I learned later, many people thought that as there are so many host families in the town, hundreds were sure to reply and so they did not get in touch with me, with the result that I received only a few phone calls. I resorted to introducing the subject of my enquiry into general conversation and this worked very well.

To help the families with their memories I gave each the following list of questions; not everybody replied to all questions.

What do you think you gained/lost from this experience?

Do you think that you made money from hosting students and how did their presence in your home affect your daily life?

Did you form any lasting friendships with the students?

Have you any special anecdote/s about students you would like to include, funny or sad?

Did you have problems with anti-student violence?

What do you think of the efforts made by the police and local authorities to protect students and curb violence?

How do you see the future of the student industry in Hastings and St Leonards?

Do you think Hastings has a particular appeal for students?

OLIVE PEDDLESDEN.

Olive must have been among the first to host overseas students in Hastings after the long period of post-war austerity began to ease.

'In 1954 I welcomed a German girl Renate. I think I was paid six pounds a week for her keep and like most host mothers at that time I treated her as a member of the family. After Renata's return to Germany she kept in touch with me and three or four years later she was once again my student-guest, later returning to London in 1965 as an au pair, which proved to be a very unhappy situation. Renata phoned me to say she had no money and asked if she could stay with me for two weeks, until her return home was due, so I welcomed her once again. At the age of 16 my younger daughter, who needed to improve her A-level German, stayed with Renata's family, near Hamburg. Renata married Jurgen and they had had a daughter who married an Italian she had met whilst she was a studying in Italy and now they have a child. I have made many trips to Germany to visit Renata and her family and they have all made the return visits. I continued to host students up until 1965.'

Olive recalls another student who was a countess, a fact that only came to light from her name on a letter. Olive said that only when she began to take two students at a time did she begin to make money and saved up enough to buy her first fridge. Since its inception Olive has been associated with the Hastings Twin Towns scheme and has exchanged visits with people in Dordrecht and continues friendships made there.

Mr T S

'My wife and I and our three young children lived in Clive Vale at the time we hosted students. Between 1969 and 1977 we welcomed many youngsters from the EF organisation. Mostly we took in girls, two at time; we thought girls would cope better with young children; our small sons just thought the girls were YUK!

One young Italian girl, who was what you may term 'a cracker', often had a crowd of both British and foreign boys following her around like lap-dogs. It was sometimes embarrassing for the poor girl, so much so that one evening we placed a hosepipe out of the bedroom window and cooled their ardour. Hysterical laughter followed and it was all taken in good part. A neighbour never liked any of our visitors. One day he was in the back garden waving his arms around and pointing at the house, we thought he was having a go at the students who were sitting at the bedroom window. We ignored him. The following day he was out there again gesturing towards the house, this went on for several days. We thought he'd gone mad. We had a long garden and I was doing some hoeing and noticed something funny about my roof - there were shiny lumps on it. I got my ladders and went up to have a look and found that dotted around the roof there were several packages wrapped in foil - the penny dropped. As most host families know, students and sandwiches hail from different planets. Crisps, chocolate, hot dogs, Coke, ice cream and burgers YES - sandwiches – NO! The lads had been throwing the foil wrapped sandwiches upwards from their bedroom window, hoping the birds would destroy the evidence. The students had not the heart to tell us they did not want sandwiches, they just dutifully took them. We confronted the students that evening, trying to keep a serious face and asked about the 'mystery packages'. Faces went very red and apologies flowed It was too much, both my wife and I laughed and the rest of the evening was taken up drawing pictures of silly seagulls with knives and forks, trying to open their 'manna from heaven'.

I think that this next event happened in the early seventies when my family was hosting two young students from Finland. My cousin and his two mates came down from Leicester at the same time; they were herded into our large garden and set up tents to camp out. On Friday night everyone was safely home and we retired to bed at about 12.30am. Just after 2am there was a knock on our bedroom door, it was one of the students beckoning me to go with him. I got up and went into his bedroom, which he shared with another student and he pointed to the ceiling; there were drips of water coming through. The steady drip became a stream, pouring over the foot of the bed. By now everyone was on the move and chaos set in, all grabbing buckets and containers, I dashed to the stopcock, obviously the tank has burst. Everyone pitched in to help and then quickly resettled for what remained of the night. After the boys went home we received a very humorous letter from the boys' parents with a small gift, a picture book of waterfalls in Finland.

We were paid for the hosting services but it came nowhere near covering the extra costs - if anything we were out of pocket. Our intention was to give young people the opportunity to live within a

British family. It was never our aim to profit; meeting people from other countries and learning from them and having our children learn was a bonus. Hopefully, they learned from us too. On many occasions we took them on holiday weekends or days out. Our children were not jealous of the students; on the contrary, our kids thought more of them than they did of us! For them it was like having big sisters or brothers and best mates rolled into one. Eventually, our work commitments became too much to entertain residential visitors. We could not have given them the time which with young people is a necessity. Over the years students came to us from many countries including France, Germany, Italy, Belgium, Switzerland, Finland and Austria. On the whole our young guests were all respectful and well behaved; we never considered them students - more of an extended family. I believe the bonds that were formed between different cultures, religions and nationalities gave us all a better understanding of what makes the world go round. The visitors' book we kept over the years is still within the family circle. Many members of our 'foreign' family came to visit us year after year, when they were holidaying in the UK. It got very wearing, watching my kids and wife saying bye-bye again and waving wet hankies. I had a few tears too - they were grand young people.'

KAY GREEN

Kay Green has not only been a hostess to overseas students but also a teacher of English as a Foreign Language, which, she thinks, has broadened her view of the industry. Kay, a published writer and poet, said that much of her life has been influenced by what she describes as the EFL factor. It would seem that as in the case of my own daughter the potential to be a teacher of English as a foreign language showed itself very early.

Kay said:
'I remember from when I was six, reading Winnie the Pooh with a student called Cristina who although a tall, dignified grown-up, had about the same reading level as me in English. Very good for my ego! I also travelled to the Isle of Wight, full of childish self-importance, as an interpreter to our student Anna-Greta. EFL teaching is a wonderful/terrible trade, depending on how vulnerable you are when you go into it. It's low-paid, insecure work. The training is of variable

quality. My initial course was 3 months of slog – some people get a TESOL certificate in a weekend, then they wonder why they can't cope in the classroom. The diploma, the professional level qualification, is beyond the pockets of many. I was lucky. I worked for a school with academic ambitions, and my boss saw me through a range of lectures and courses, and when the time was right, paid for a diploma course. I went into the work because I love language, and it was a good choice for that but it was also a mine of insights and experiences about the world and what's going on. An example: The day of the Twin Towers disaster in New York, I went in to work to discuss the morning papers with my class which included Japanese, Italian, French, Nigerian and South American adult students. The range of feelings, ideas, and expected consequences we discussed took me far, far further than anything I could have learned from the papers.'

Kay said that she did not make money from hosting students, She also believes that her years of teaching English as a foreign language have given her the opportunity to hear the other side of host-family situations.

'I think, at the rates most schools offer, you'd have to have several students to a room, and feed them cheaply to profit financially. (Judging from the whinging about 'English food' I heard from my students in class, quite a few people do this when they need some cash). As a host family we took only one or two students at a time, for 6-12 weeks of the year, and regarded them as a novelty and as an excuse to buy wine with the meal, and do tours of local places of interest at the weekend, so we spent what we were given, and joined in the fun. We made one or two lasting friendships with students; quite a lot exchanged letters for a while, one or two came back for a private visit the next year. One in particular sticks in my mind, a Japanese woman who was studying to teach Japanese to English and American businessmen, at the time when I was studying to teach business English. We gained enormously from studying and practising together. She came to us for Christmas the next winter, bringing a friend with her, and we all exchanged letters and tapes, and she visited several times more during the following 10 years.

Occasionally there was a loss of privacy or time wasted in arrangements but it was negligible next to the gains in cultural and personal ideas our family experienced and adopted. I think the potential gains in tolerance and mental agility brought about by mixing with a range of people are a cure for so many of the wrong-headed ideas modern Britain suffers from. And for our family in particular, I am an only child, as is my daughter so the experience of different kinds of people coming into the family was, I think, a great antidote to the shyness and aloofness that only-children are prone to. The most obvious gain is our stock of useful phrases in about ten languages, but it goes much further than that. Here are some random examples of attitudes we gathered from our students:

Japan: Rice is a good breakfast food. Wearing outdoor shoes on the carpet is stupid. When you're really stressed, have a wash then a bath, then a shower. There is nothing that cannot be said politely, if you only think before you speak.

Sweden: What has relaxed nudity got to do with sex?

France: There's nothing wrong with cheap food or cheap clothes, as long as you use them imaginatively.

Italy and the Mediterranean: Laughing, crying, screaming, extravagant declarations of love, hugs, kisses and back-slapping are all good means of family communication – even between men.

Arab states: Alcohol is a potentially dangerous drug, which can cause just as much grief and evil as heroin.

Korea: If you are lucky enough to know what you want, don't dream. Be single-minded, and work like billy-oh until you get it.

Mexico: Don't worry.

My daughter grew up around a range of mysterious characters, including Corinne from Paris, who had never experienced ready-meals, reverently telling everyone my husband was a wonderful cook, and writing back after her visit wanting the recipe for 'fish-fingers'…Days of mystery when Henrich, the Danish giant insisted that English landlords and shopkeepers kept saying 'cheese pie' to him, and we insisted that they did not. During the next few days, Henrich even reported back on a lesson that included Cockney Rhyming Slang. "Obviously," he declared, "cheese pie must be slang for 'goodbye'!" We didn't believe him. The mystery continued. It was eventually solved when my husband took a phone call, and Henrich jumped from his chair shouting; "That's it! You said it then!" – My husband had finished the call with the words, "Cheers, bye!"'

Kay thought that street violence against students is a reliable indicator of the social state of the town, suggesting that is it worse in Hastings, a relatively poor town, than it is in Bath or Bournemouth;   She said:

'Anti-student violence was not often a problem in the 70s – which was an easy time to be a teenager, as I remember it. We youngsters regarded the students as a fact of life: occasionally annoying, occasionally interesting – but with terrible fashion-sense. (Just different, actually, but that's teen thinking for you!)

By contrast, in the 90s there was more poverty and unemployment, and local youths had much less patience with visitors generally, and students in particular. There were some nasty incidents, and as teachers we were constantly warning our charges to go about in groups, to get taxis late at night and so on. We felt for the students, and on the odd occasion when disputes went their way we were wickedly proud. My favourite example was Rafael, a reckless, bright-eyed young Polish man, who had a few more beers than was good for him one night, and, finding a dispute developing between the Europeans and the South Americans he was out with, he launched into a lecture on togetherness. Unfortunately, beer and enthusiasm for oratory got the better of him, and he found himself persuading them that they, as foreigners, should stick together and give the Brits what-for. The next minute, 25 or so cheering, yelling students burst upon the unsuspecting town centre calling for reinforcements as they went, and mayhem ensued. It took us a long time to extract this story from the bruised and shamefaced crowd of students that arrived at school the next day, saying they had hangovers and didn't want to talk about it!

There were examples which left we shepherds of students feeling that rough justice had occurred: One was when a bunch of local vandals had got too sure of students being an easy target, and attempted to mug what turned out to be half of a Bolivian football team. Bolivia won. The police convinced the offenders that, "He hit me just because I was trying to nick his wallet" wasn't a sensible thing to say in court, and charges were dropped. I feel that disturbances in the town generally are worse when there is less police presence. My perception is that over the years, the police presence has become less widespread, and less communicative – but now I do not spend much time in town in the evenings. My daughter says the police are there now – but that it's hard to talk to riot-vans, so there's not much communication. I remember my bosses taking part in 'Operation Columbus' activities, but I wasn't directly involved so don't know much about the project.'

Commentingon the standards of boarding and teaching of students Kay said:

'It varies enormously, and has been a remarkably unregulated industry. I have worked in a small, ambitious school that was family-run. They lived on site, treated their teachers like family, and their host-families like honoured associates. I have worked in a summer 'student factory' where everything is churned through at the least possible cost, and teachers and students alike are permanently dizzy and sometimes in danger. Lack of regulation leads to accidents, but it also allows for creativity, and the unlikely friendships and collaborations I have seen spring up around the schools and boarding houses which often seemed to me to make the more chaotic elements well worthwhile.'

Asked about her view of the future of the language school industry Kay replied:

'I think things are becoming more regulated, in the sense that there are more inspections and more rules. I'm not convinced this is entirely a good thing: Determined swindlers are always good at dodging regulations, and a demand for more qualifications will actually deprive the industry of some of the more interesting teachers – those who teach in their gap-year from university, for example, and the many writers, artists and travellers who fill in by teaching from time to time.

A few years ago, the word was that language-travel would be rendered obsolete by online courses, but people still like to travel and get the cultural experience as well. Hastings is not so much a centre for the student industry as it once was, though. Not being closely involved any more, I don't know why. However, I think Hastings has particular appeal for students; it's relatively small, within reach of London, and is well-stocked with pub-entertainers, musicians and oddball characters that are excellent material for travellers' tales. Hastings is not smart or cosmopolitan, but that often leaves visitors feeling they've been to a 'real' place. I don't remember any of my students saying Hastings is acceptable. They always either loved or hated it,'

DONNA

'We didn't have students every summer when I was a child, only maybe three or four years. I always enjoyed it when we did, because it was exciting always having someone new in the house. Talking to the students gave me a broader idea of how very different each person's lifestyle was from my own. I was usually shy of them when they arrived but upset to see them go, (this may have had something to do with decreasing language difficulties).

I became very used to people from many different nationalities - most, but not all, European. Possibly because I was around them from such a young age, it never crossed my mind to have prejudices against them. One thing that definitely influenced my attitude to foreigners was my mother teaching in a language school. Most of my friends have at some point made derogatory remarks about people from certain cultures, whilst I was getting to know them personally on a day to day basis. I am very glad I had this closer experience with other nationalities.

I never had any cause to feel jealous of the students, because they were treated as, and for the most part acted as, part of the family, all spending some time together, and some time apart. We routinely had meals together and occasionally went out together, but they were usually busy studying or on day-trips, so I still had plenty of time alone with my parents.

I was aware of a higher standard of living when the students were there – we had a great choice of breakfast foods, for example. That was the main benefit. I disliked the fact that I didn't feel so free in my own home - there may always be someone watching, or someone who could be offended. Often there would be someone who spent hours in our one and only bathroom! In fact, my dad rigged up an emergency toilet in the garage, just in case! (Thankfully it was never used.) But then, this was all probably good for me as, being an only child, I didn't often have to share my space with others.

We are no longer in contact with any of the students, but as a family we remained in contact with some for a little while. We exchanged cards and gifts at Christmas, and one came back to stay with us for her holiday. There were one or two closer friendships between my mother and some of her ex-students, with one in particular doing a "meal-exchange" with us - she came to us for Christmas Dinner, and a few weeks later, came back and cooked us a traditional Japanese meal! That was interesting, and the experience was enjoyable if not the food.

I remember several language-misunderstandings that caused long-term family jokes! For example, the French girl announcing loudly, "I am angry" My parents tried in vain to figure out how they had upset her, before discovering that she was attempting to say "hungry". I don't have any very interesting anecdotes, just several small memories. The Austrian girl who unfortunately spent her entire stay on the sofa because she had a terrible cold and didn't want to irritate her room-mate, the time my mum accidentally (although it didn't look like it) threw a spaghetti Bolognese at the Belgian girl, the anxiety when the German girl lost her purse (which was actually handed in by the person who found it, in the end!) and my amazement at discovering the student who lived in what to me seemed like a castle.

The buried cabbage story really is pretty much what it sounds like. At a party where all the guests were of different nationalities, someone brought a portion of traditional food from Korea. They take a whole cabbage, wrap it up and bury it just below the freezing soil in the winter, and leave it for several weeks to ferment. Once fermented, they mix it with other foods and eat it. I think this is a variation of Sauerkraut, but I had not heard of it and found it rather shocking.'

NETTIE

'When I decided to have students it was for the money I could earn, whilst staying at home to look after my own children, I also realised these students, some of them quite young, needed a home that felt like home, even if it was only for a few weeks and I wanted to look after them as I would hope someone in another country would look after my children. I had many students pass through my home and am pleased to say 99% of them were lovely. I began taking students in 1976 and only stopped completely in 2005. In that time there have been many memorable ones: The French girl who came for a few months in 1978, her family then invited us back to their home, which I declined as we had four sons and the idea of staying in someone else's home could have been a nightmare, but they insisted we come and said we could put up our tent in their garden as there was plenty of room. We decided to go and armed with tent arrived at their home, only to find it was a chateau. We knew the French student's father worked in a L'Armagnac distillery, we didn't know he owned it and most of the village; consequently we had a wonderful holiday. We did put up our tents in the very large garden and there were toilets and showers in an extension to the garage. We also got to sample the L'Armagnac. In fact we had many holidays in their garden. The student's father is now the mayor of the village and we are still friends.

There was a Turkish boy who arrived and could not speak one word of English. Within one month he had learnt so much and could understand almost everything. Whilst in Hastings, he met a Swiss girl, who was also a student and much to our surprise they continued their relationship after leaving Hastings. They eventually married and live in Switzerland with their 2 sons. We have had many holidays with them. He says he learnt most of his early English from our boys when he offered to read stories to them and because they would laugh when he made a mistake and correct him.

A young Austrian married couple, who came for 1 month and despite the fact I was supposed to be looking after them, helped me out considerably, as my 8 year old son was in hospital with a broken arm and leg after an accident and my 5 year old son was in hospital having

*his tonsils removed. They would look after the other children whilst I
visited the hospital and wash up after dinner, which was really
appreciated at that time. We have since been able to repay them by
having their sons on visits when they were old enough to learn English,
and we are still good friends.*

*We also had many German students; there was one who insisted he had
to have Tabasco sauce on anything he ate, even his desserts, and
another who wanted to try Marmite. I explained it had a very strong
taste and he must only put a little on his toast, but he spread it very
thickly, like jam, I did try to warn him and as he took his first bite he
knew he should have listened. I said, 'leave it if you don't like it', but
no, he bravely battled through it then quickly left the table. He never
touched the Marmite again.*

*We hosted an 11 year old boy, who arrived in 1978; he was very
confident, tall blonde and loud but very nice, we took him out with us
a lot as he was only a little older than our own children. He came back
to stay with us repeatedly and when he was old enough he came over
to Hastings and worked in a restaurant for the summer, to improve his
English. Of course he stayed with us; he calls us his English mum and
dad. He's now married with children and although we don't see him so
much he rings often, he brought his family over to London recently and
we met him there for the weekend.*

*When the Berlin Wall was taken down we started having people from
East Germany. It was interesting to listen to the older generation
talking about life behind the wall; they all learnt Russian but were
trying very hard to master English. Four ladies in their 60's came to
stay; they had a programme of visits to make whilst they were here; it
tired me out just to read what they were going to do. But each morning,
bright and early, they set off, sometimes not getting back until late.
They wanted to see and do everything which had been denied them.*

*We also hosted the English teacher from a school in East Germany.
They began bringing pupils over every year for 10 years. We have
obviously become very good friends over the years and we were very
disappointed when the school was closed down. It was also the end of
my years of taking in students.*

Only once did I ever have to complain to the leaders; when I had two Swedish boys, aged 13, who thought it would be fun to drink vodka all the time. They were not happy with me when I didn't approve. The leaders had a word with them and they didn't drink in front of me again but were terribly rude and the only ones I was pleased to see the back of. I enjoyed my time taking in students and through it have friends all over Europe. We are still hearing from some who only spent 3 weeks with us over 20 years ago.'

MRS JAMES

Mrs James began hosting students in 1969. They were supplied by a small language school in High Wickham, Hastings; the students tended to be young and of various nationalities. When this organisation closed she took students from a large, international company. Mrs James' motivation in becoming a host mother was to add to the family income, while remaining at home to bring up her five daughters. She always treated her students as family and felt that having overseas guests stretched her mind, with the challenges of helping them with their language problems and prompting her to think up new recipes and entertainments. Her own children adapted well to having students in the house.

Mrs James has strong recollections of particular students:

'A big German boy called Gunter arrived with an enormous suitcase containing practically all his clothes, as his mother feared there would be nobody to do his washing. Gunter proved to be very practical and one day he volunteered to help my husband dig the garden. Having no work boots with him Gunter wrapped his shod feet in plastic bags. For less happy reasons I recall a Japanese man who thought that host mother meant servant and expected to be waited on hand and foot. However, he did do his own laundry but upset me by hanging the wet garments in the trees and bushes in the garden. I stopped hosting in the early 1990s. It seems to me that there are fewer students in Hastings these days but I think that the town still has considerable appeal for them because of its history and that there are lots of attractions for young people in Hastings and it is close to London.'

BERNADETTE JAMES

Mrs James' eldest daughter, Bernadette, who is an EFL and Modern Foreign Languages teacher in a local school, also hosted students while her children were small. Bernadette lived and worked abroad before motherhood.

'I have always enjoyed talking with people from other countries and having them as guests. Sometimes it was bit irksome to be obliged to prepare and cook big meals, when the family and I would have preferred to have eaten more simply but the bonus was that the students were often delighted to find a baby or toddler in the house and they made good baby-watchers.

My career as a part time EFL teacher began when I was a student. By the age of 25 I was overseeing the assessment of large, weekly intakes of students in the summer months. These were the boom years of the student industry in Hastings and St Leonards and it was almost impossible to cope with the demand for teaching and accommodation. Teaching staff were given only two hours to test and categorise almost 100 students, according to their level of English. Language classes, sometimes conducted by teachers with dubious qualifications, took place throughout the day from 9.00am to 6.00pm, which put pressure on everybody, including the host families. I heard about the violence perpetrated upon students by locals from the students and while in no way excusing it I think that the students were not always sensible in their conduct and did not heed the good advice they were given about public behaviour. Especially in the matter of flaunting their possessions in public and attracting attention to themselves, by noisy or socially provocative behaviour. I was also made aware of the widely differing standards of hospitality the students received from their host families. Some students, on learning how little the families were paid, were astonished at the welcoming and generous treatment they received. Others complained that there were up to 10 students in the house, that they had to eat separately from the host family and were give different and inferior food. I think that the mass arrivals of students seen in the 70s and 80s are a thing of the past but there will always be people who need to learn English, so the industry will continue in the town but in a modified way.'

Bernadette said she has kept in touch with some of her students and retains regular contact with a Swiss girl and a German girl. Bernadette concluded by saying that that Hastings' coastal location and its closeness to cities and historic sites will always give it a special attraction for students.

MR B

Former police officer Mr B and his wife hosted overseas students during the late 1960s, which gave him an unusual perspective on the industry as both a former upholder of the law and a host family. I have deliberately preserved the formal style of English that Mr B, now in his nineties, used in his beautifully hand-written accounts of his role as host father.

'In the early 1950s foreign students from former enemy countries suffered some hostility from British teenagers - assaults and robberies became fairly frequent and required special attention from the police. Some years later it became customary for the student agencies to provide their students with distinctively patterned haversacks and this practice provided an easy means of identifying the agency responsible for the students and unfortunately picking them out as targets for violence. I recall some difficulties arising from foreign students refusing to queue properly at bus stops and several cases arose from them being roughly handled in consequence. Students used coffee bars as favourite meeting places and student identity cards entitled the owners to reduced fares on trains and public transport and cheaper tickets in cinemas, theatres and sports centres.

I had the sad task of dealing with the tragic deaths of two German students. They were camping at Galley Hill in a steel framed tent. During a severe thunderstorm the tent was struck by lightning, killing both. The return of their bodies to Germany presented some difficulties at first, as their parents refused to pay the expenses involved. From the 1950s onwards the fees paid to local householders for the accommodation of students became an essential factor in improving the local economy and in many cases maintained solvency. The total of the local unemployed was depressingly high and the town's economy was only very slowly recovering from the effects of WWII.

In 1967 my wife and I had a three bed-roomed bungalow, and because our son had won a scholarship to Oxford University and our daughter was working and living abroad, two bedrooms were unused. We contacted a student's residence agency in St Leonards and our offer to accommodate foreign students was welcomed after an inspection of our home. We were given printed instructions as follows:

Hosts should collect their allotted students arriving in coaches at Falaise Road, Hastings from 10.00pm onwards.
Students should be provided with breakfast, lunch, (or packed lunch) tea and supper. Students should attend class 9.00am to 12.00pm daily.

Occasionally they would have coach outings, attend a cinema or theatre, jazz concert, dances, etc. There was a strict rule that students attending dances should return home to their lodgings by 11.30pm. Students would play tennis at either White Rock Gardens or Alexandra Park, cricket at South Saxons Fields, football at Bexhill Road Recreation Ground. Hosts were expected to wash and iron the students' clothing and to assist and encourage them to become fluent in English. It was customary for the parents of students being accommodated to give their hostess a gift on their arrival at their lodgings. We had foreign students living with us for over three years and generally this was a very harmonious experience. They usually came on a three or four week's course. I can recall only the memorable incidents concerning foreign students who stayed with us. Our first guests were a postgraduate from a Japanese university and two students from Hanover. The Japanese was always very polite and respectful. He had a limited English vocabulary but could read English quite well. His first remark on being shown his bedroom was, 'Me Japanese, very sorry, war no good.' We assured him we understood the reason for his discomfort, but we pointed out that his two companions were Germans and also from an enemy country. The Japanese soon settled down and studied the books and newspapers I supplied him with. He discussed these with me and listened intently to the BBC radio. Our second guests were a Finnish deputy hotel manager and two vivacious Swedish girls. All three could speak English fairly well and made good progress in their vocabulary. The studious Finn was rather concerned about the girls' free and easy behaviour. I am still in regular touch with this Finn, he married and had a family and is now retired and regularly spends holidays on the Canary Islands.

Another student whose company we enjoyed was Peter from Munich. He was a jovial youth; at his first breakfast he sampled bread spread with our homemade strawberry jam; he enjoyed this so much that he had three slices. We complied with Peter's request that he be supplied with two slices of bread and jam after a substantial lunch and again with his tea and supper. This happened every day and we were able to maintain Peter's ecstasy about our strawberry jam until his departure for Germany three weeks later. We had two memorable German students – undergraduates from a university. One was a trainee dentist and the other a trainee doctor. It was obvious from the day of their arrival that they intended to take full advantage of their month's course in English. Both were fluent and could read the language well. They concentrated on completing the course work set by their tutors and frequently sought my advice on questions and usage of the language. When they had finished their homework, like the Japanese student, they listened to BBC radio talks and also invited me to listen to their readings from newspapers and the works of Charles Dickens and to correct any mispronunciations, if necessary. They learnt I was a St John's Ambulance Service first-aider and we had some very interesting discussions about that discipline. A first-aid manual and medical encyclopedia were very helpful in these discussions. At the end of their course and stay with us the pair bade us a very fond farewell and thanked my wife and I for all the kind assistance we had given them to attain maximum marks in their course assessment.

Some three years later the trainee doctor called at our house with his fiancée. They were enjoying a cycling holiday in southern England. They stayed for lunch with us and I learned that my former student intended to enlist in the German Army Medical Corp to do his National Service. About two years later we were delighted to hear that he had passed his first medical exams; initially he was a partner in a surgery near his house and subsequently he had his own practice. The student who shared his accommodation with him in our home eventually qualified and had his own dental practice. In contrast to these two happy relationships there was a drastic difference in another student. His first demand on arriving at our home was. 'Where are my bottles of water? Hastings water - no good.' We assured him that our mains water supply was excellent and my wife and I each drank a glass but this failed to convince the youth that Hastings water is perfect and he was misinformed. His rejoinder was, 'All my water must be boiled!' (It never was). Another student was a pleasant and studious type: He had an ambition to secure a place at a university and we assisted him in his course home work and fluency. We took him to Oxford to see our son's M. A. graduation in modern languages and then for a tour of some of the famous colleges; this all seemed to inspire him to greater effort.

Several unfortunate incidents marred our usual good experience of hosting students. One involved an ex-member of the Hitler Youth; an aggressive and impolite person. On the journey from Germany he had quarrelled with his companion and was not on speaking terms with him when they arrived. We tried to reconcile them without success. On the second morning of their stay with us there was a fracas between them. This resulted in a window being broken and a lamp fitting damaged. I immediately ordered the aggressor to pack his belongings and the student agency transferred him elsewhere and paid for the damage. It was customary for me to advise our students to behave in an orderly and sensible manner with their peers and the general public. One of the students I so advised replied, 'I am a boxer and will deal with anyone looking for a fight'. Such talk as this caused me some concern. At this time, on Friday and Saturday nights a dance was organised for students on Hastings Pier, These events were always very popular. The dances terminated at 11.00pm and a service of buses was supplied for the students, who were expected to be back at their accommodation by 11.30pm. One Saturday night my wife and I were waiting at 11.30pm for the return of the "boxer" student who had told us he was attending the dance at the pier. He had not returned by midnight and we were becoming anxious about him. At 12.30pm I telephoned Hastings Police to check if there was any news of our missing youth or if he had been involved in an accident. The police replied that our subject had been involved in a fight at the pier and was detained in the accident and emergency department of the Royal East Sussex Hospital. I immediately drove to the hospital and found that our student was being treated for a fractured nose, a black eye, three loosened teeth and a cracked rib. He was discharged at 1.30am and I drove him home. I ascertained from the police officer dealing with the incident that our student had insulted and threatened to knock down a peaceful and law abiding coloured youth, who had promptly landed his aggressor with several effective punches and fled the scene. The following day I arranged for our student's loosened teeth to be treated by a dentist. For over a week the patient had to subsist on a liquid diet and his studies were limited.

We had the pleasure of accommodating three jolly Austrian Girl Guides – all very fit and outdoor types. They were experienced campers and very interested in our accounts of extensive touring by car and camping all over the UK and the Continent. There was a prolonged spell of warm and sunny weather at this time and the trio decided to organise a series of camp-fire picnics on the beach at Glyne Gap. I loaned them all the necessary camping and cooking equipment and the girls walked several times along the beach from Galley Hill to Bo-peep, collecting driftwood in sacks. We provided them with food suitable for a camp-fire picnic; sausages, baking potatoes, bacon, baked beans, etc. The girls had become great friends with a spaniel dog, who was delighted to go with them on these adventures and to swim in the sea with them.

During one particular period of our association with students there occurred a number of cases of students being assaulted and robbed. As a precaution we advised our guests to strictly limit the cash they took out and to leave the balance of their money with us for safe keeping. This advice was usually acted upon, with one exception: a defiant youth always carried with him his total of cash in a wallet/purse. He had the misfortune of being assaulted by four teenagers and was robbed of £150.00. The thieves were never arrested and the victim had to telegraph his parents in Hanover for a replacement of the stolen money.

I still have vivid memory of a sad incident involving a German student: On arriving at our home he produced his booking document for my inspection. I read this aloud as was customary. I said, 'Peter Langsborff, I remember Captain Langsborff of the Graf Spee, the German battleship.' The student, standing to attention, replied, 'Yes Sir, he was my uncle.' He had tears running down his cheeks. 'He was an honourable and humane officer, I am sorry he is dead.' I shook the boy's hand and he recovered his composure and shook mine. He spent a happy time with us.

73

It was fairly common for students detailed to us not to be provided by their parents with a mackintosh or raincoat for use during rain. In consequence of this, the students concerned were obliged to buy such a necessary garment. One student, living with us during a particularly rainy spell, had arrived without waterproof clothing and consequently, several times he came home soaking wet. He refused to buy a mackintosh and I decided to loan him an old waterproof from my garden shed. He seemed unconcerned about his shabby and disreputable appearance whilst wearing this garment!

Our association with boarding foreign students came to an end when our established student agency closed down. Generally speaking we enjoyed the company of the students and we assisted them to the best of our ability. All of them sincerely thanked us for our kindness and attention to them. It is gratifying to know that in a very minor way we helped to foster good international relations.'

VAL RELFE

'In July 1976, a tall, 16 year old German boy named Wolfgang, arrived at our home in Briers Avenue, Hastings, for a two week holiday. Wolfgang came from Worringen, a suburb of Cologne; the visit was arranged by a fellow member of his church choir, who had been a student-guest of a neighbour the previous year. Wolfgang, who resembled Boris Becker, was a somewhat brash and noisy youth, a common characteristic of Rhinelanders. We discovered that we shared a sense of humour and he was very keen to improve his English. Wolfgang loved to chat with my husband late into the night, over a pot of tea. They discussed many subjects, including politics and world affairs, with Wolfgang working hard to improve his vocabulary and pronunciation. I remember thinking at the time that Wolfgang's father and mine had fought on opposite sides during the war. Wolfgang was dismayed at our breakfast of toast and cereal, as many Germans eat meat for breakfast; in fact meat is a much greater part of their diet than it is for the British. On subsequent visits he brought his own sausage and beer, creating a little Germany in my house. I had many other students in the following five years until we moved to Uckfield.

I found the Italians tended to suffer from homesickness and were very difficult to please, when it came to food. One Italian girl decided to live on cream crackers for the duration of her visit. The lunch pack of sandwiches was always a problem and the kind of filling I enjoyed, for example Marmite and lettuce, was regarded as disgusting. I once discovered a packet of sandwiches that had been posted down the back of the wardrobe in the student's room. Wolfgang made a number of return visits to us and our friendship grew and flourished and later included his girlfriend, Andrea, whom he married. We were present at their engagement, wedding and the first Communion of their twin daughters (now 14) and have shared holidays with them.

We have hosted Wolfgang's parents, parents-in-law and assorted other relatives. They have welcomed to their homes our sons, my husband's nephews and niece and many of our friends. Wolfgang's influence on the next generation has been most notable with my husband's nephew, Mike, who studied A level German. Prior to going to university, he spent 6 months working for a print firm in Dusseldorf, and readily admits that he would have struggled if it had not been for the support and presence of Wolfgang and his wife, Andrea, who often invited him to spend weekends with them and gave him a chance to speak English. The following year, during the university holidays, Mike worked for 4 weeks at Wolfgang's firm Dupont, in Wuppertal. He stayed with the family and travelled to work with Wolfgang. This was at the time of the 2002 World Cup and Wolfgang, (a great football fan), was particularly irked if he had to miss an important match, while waiting for Mike to finish a shift. Mike's sister, Becky, also went on to study A level German, as she wanted to be able to communicate with Wolfgang's daughters.

Overall, I did make some money during the years I hosted students but not a great deal; just enough to help towards family holidays. I never experienced problems with violence from locals towards my students but it was not that prevalent in the 1970s. I can understand the appeal of Hastings to students, especially Germans, who have so few coastal towns; they seem particularly fond of the Old Town.'

CRIS KENNARD

'I started hosting students in 1979 with one Swiss girl and I have only had one break when my first husband died in 1983; then I took three years out. I have gained many friendships over the years and still exchange cards and notes with an Italian girl, (she's a woman of 45 now) I had an invitation to her wedding but couldn't go. She wrote to me about adopting 2 children and the break up of her marriage. An Italian student boy came back to visit with a friend one year and camped in the garden, as I had family staying with me. This caused a stir with the neighbours as their female students watched from the window as the boys did their morning exercises on the lawn.

We have had all cultures staying with us, including Muslims. One used to put his prayer mat on the landing as it faced east. We forgot to tell a friend of my daughter to go up stairs slowly and the poor boy fell over the Arab boy, I don't know who was more surprised the Arab at seeing a big 6ft coming at him or our friend having to jump pretty quickly. This particular Arab used to change into a long white robe when he arrived back from college and loved making tea; he always went out in a smart suit and white shirt even in the hot weather. He was from a wealthy family and had a list of items to buy for his return home, mainly handbags for his aunts and Marks and Spencer grey duffle coats for his younger siblings. His bathroom habits were a little annoying as he had to rise very early and wash under running water, before saying his prayers. One vegetarian boy put evaporated milk on his cabbage, thinking it was a fine English sauce and continued to eat it, even after realising it was to go with the fruit at the end of the meal. We still can't eat cabbage without talking about it. (We can't bring ourselves to even try it.)

One German boy walked into the wrong house as we share a driveway with next door, he opened the door and rushed in as he had forgotten his bus ticket. My neighbour jumped out of his chair thinking it was a burglar, his dog went mad and the poor boy fled. He never told us what he had done but my neighbour came round to see if he was OK. He was also pleased it reminded him that he had left his keys in the front door. The same lad also took a wrong turning one evening and was chased by a dog; he jumped into another neighbour's garden and could see

76

our house from there, so he thought he would just climb over the fences; he was seen and had a bit of explaining to do.

Problems with violence don't happen very often in this part of town (upper St. Leonards) but one incident we remember happened to our students and two other German boys, who were staying down our road. They were returning home about 9-30pm so it wasn't late, when a group of English boys with sticks confronted them. One student managed to get away and called us out. We went to investigate and said we had called the police and that they were on their way. At that moment my son and his friend drove up and said, 'What's the problem?' We shouted out that the lads in hoodies were being aggressive and to follow them. The hoodies obviously thought they were plain-clothed police officers and ran in all directions; all we could do was laugh. There still seems to be violence towards foreigners in certain areas of the town, the police do what they can but can't be everywhere.

There will always be visitors to Hastings as 1066 is in all history books and it is easy to travel to London and other cities of interest. We have had Brazilians and Russian students who have taken trips to Paris for weekends as we are so close to France.'

PHILIP - A TAXI DRIVER. A PARTICULAR VIEW

Taxi drivers gain a particular view of the community in which they work. One evening in the summer of 2006, I was being driven to a meeting by one of our local cabbies when we passed a large group of students gathered on a narrow pathway of All Saints Street. My driver muttered, 'Students!' as they jostled dangerously on the pavement. I said to him that he sounded as if he had some strong views about them and I would like to hear more of what he thought. I spoke to him a few days later, expecting a tirade against students but he was surprisingly sympathetic.

'I sometimes wonder if these kids know what they are letting themselves in for, as far as their accommodation is concerned. Some of the addresses where I drop them off look like hovels - dirty, run-down places; for example there's a road in the West Hill area. The other

night I picked up two Czech girls from their coach arrival point on the seafront at St Leonards, and drove to them to their host family via Filsham Road. I was aware of the girls exclaiming at the lovely houses they passed and noticed their disappointment when I dropped them at a rather seedy looking house in Silverhill. I feel sure that most host families only take students to make money and that it is not only in the low standard of accommodation that the students are exploited. I have picked up local people from a local frozen food market who boast openly of the cheap food they have bought to feed the students. I also think that students should be taught the rules of the road and about the way of life here, as their ignorance puts them in danger.'

I assured Philip that all decent schools do instruct the students on road safety and British customs and this is often reinforced by the host families' advice and that cases of inferior accommodation and food offered to students are in the minority.

CHAPTER FIVE

FACTS AND FIGURES

Towards the end of the summer of 2003 I was approached by university student Naomi Gotts who was working on a dissertation entitled, 'Perceptions and Attitudes of Hastings Residents towards Foreign Language Students'. She had prepared a four page questionnaire, which she was circulating among the general public in the months of August and September, when the peak of the student season had just ended and the memory of large numbers of students in the town was still fresh. Additionally, and to provide balance, Naomi spoke to students and staff of language schools, which is where I made my own contribution. Although it was several years since I had been active in the industry Naomi felt I still had something relevant to add. I was particularly interested in her survey because I had already conceived the idea of this book.

For the initial research for her dissertation, Naomi hand-delivered 480 questionnaires in three different streets in every local electoral ward, selecting the first ten houses in each street. From this source she received 129 responses. The questionnaire was also put online and advertised to people via email, web forums and in an article in the local newspaper, producing 31 responses. To raise the response rate from young people of Hastings to the questionnaire it was given to Year 12 students at a local sixth form, which gained another 63 responses. These different approaches resulted in 223 responses for analysis. The responders to the questionnaire were predominantly female. I have no specialist knowledge of response rate to surveys but this result strikes me as impressive and an indication of how important to Hastings residents are the issues surrounding overseas students.

Naomi's dissertation is necessarily academic and I have attempted to translate the data into a narrative. Overall, the survey highlighted the differences in the level of acceptance of students between people who had direct contact with students and those who did not. It should not be surprising to find that people who have a close association with students or stood to benefit from their presence in the town should regard it more favourably. It seemed, too, that the older generation are more kindly disposed towards students, except for those who complained of them being noisy and overcrowding public footpaths and transport. The responses to the questionnaire by the members of a local sixth form were very pertinent. This is the age group (but not this particular social group, I must add) who commit much of the crime against students. The sixth formers disagreed that the students enhance the local residents' spirit of hospitality and thought that there is a general feeling of hostility towards students by locals. They thought that the students contribute to the litter in the town, are noisy and rude, create overcrowding in public areas and on transport and that there are too many students in Hastings. If you apply the sixth formers' objections to the presence of overseas students to a similarly aged, local social group, one that already feels deprived - by lack of money, education or proper parental support - it is easy to see how street violence against the students is engendered.

This is by no means just a present day problem. Elsewhere in this book a retired police officer, who hosted overseas students over 30 years ago says,

'In the early 1950s, students from former enemy countries suffered some hostility from British teenagers; assault and robberies became fairly frequent and required special attention from the police.'

It should not be thought that hostility to students is solely a Hastings and St Leonards problem. When I first had access to the Internet, in my last year of work with the language school, I frequently searched the online versions of Sussex and Kent local newspapers for anti-student crime reports. I discovered that in towns that are considered select and well-to-do, violence against overseas students occurred; even in Tunbridge Wells, that supposed bastion of middle-aged respectability.

Some of the responses Naomi received from a Hastings sixth form class to her questions about their feelings towards overseas students were:

Alice: *'I do feel displaced by students on the buses. And they are very*

recognizable too because they walk around with identical, brightly coloured hats and bags.'

Alice wrote about the street violence against the students.

'The students are not blameless. When I get dressed up to go into town for an evening I'll be walking along in the town and I get comments thrown at me from students. It's not very nice having that happen at all but especially from the students.'

Ben: *'I was in the cinema one time and there was a group of students there too and they were screaming and shouting and throwing popcorn around, which was very annoying.'*

Ben also thought that the students should bear some responsibility for the attacks.

'It always seems to be the case that whenever there is an incident the students will never get blamed, it always seems the local people who are blamed for the attacks, even where it was the other way round - students attacking locals.'

Phillip: *'It's not the taking over space part that that can get annoying. It's the noise they make; they are very loud and very recognizable because they are shouting in a language you can't understand.'*

Phillip wanted to correct the impression that it was only the students who get attacked.

'I was walking into to town once with a couple of my mates, when a student started shouting abuse at us. Then they started attacking us and there was a fight. I almost got a bottle thrown at my head.'

Phillip agreed with Alice on the tendency of male students to shout out at local girls.

'I think that's one of the reasons there have been so many attacks –incidents like that. If you are walking along in town with your

girlfriend and students start shouting comments at her then you feel you have to stand up for and protect her. Some students need to show a bit more respect. They're over here, in a different country and need to respect the people here more.'

My work in a language school has been predominantly with Italian students and certainly this nationality is noisy, in private and public, a characteristic that can grate in a quiet, English, coastal/semi-rural town. When in Italy I found the contrast between the gentle hum of conversation in a British restaurant or bank and the noisy chatter of those in Italy irritating.

Naomi interviewed language school staff on the subject of crimes against students.

Summer Language School Centre Manger and Teacher .

'For our school it's a major problem, especially in the summer when we get children in. I'd say in my role as centre manager, during a week, three out of five days, there's an incident reported to me and then there's the incidents that the students don't tell anybody about. This summer we've had students attacked by knives, with baseball bats, students punched and hit on the beach. I get students coming in and asking, 'what does **** mean?' You ask them how they know that word and they'll tell you someone called them that name the other day. They'll be told to get back to their own country a lot, and it's usually students who are recognizably foreign. The Latin Americans say that their attackers are about their own age. I'd say usually between 16 to 25 years.'

Language School Representative.

'Attacks on students are a big problem and can have a marked effect on the student concerned, particularly if there has been an element of violence and this will mar the student's impression of his stay in Hastings.'

In recent years my daughter has included in her preparations for Italian students booked for the course in Hastings, basic instruction in English swear words. Some Italian parents who speak English have been shocked by this but have come to accept that is a safety measure, enabling the student who is confronted to be able to understand if they under threat. But it could just as well exacerbate the situation if the overseas student knows a collection of English swear words. Anyhow, as we know, when first learning a foreign language, youngsters are always intrigued by the profanities in a different tongue. So it's not such a departure teaching these words, which the students might well come to know by other means.

Students' Experiences of Hastings.

Naomi thought it was important to find out how the overseas students felt about Hastings and so conducted group interviews at two of the town's language schools with students aged 16 and over.

Isabella: '*There are too many English people fighting and drinking beer. It is too expensive here and the free bus finishes too early. Taxis are expensive.*'

Sophie: '*It is very dangerous here.*'

Daryl: '*Other students tell me that Hastings is not such a peaceful place. Sometimes the young English people say. 'Give me your money' or something like that. But compared with Bournemouth for me it is a peaceful place.*'

Michaela: '*You mean Hastings is peaceful?*'

Daryl: '*Yes.*'

Michaela: '*Well, sometimes I am made fun of by local people, the teenagers. Maybe they get drunk sometimes. I was called Chinese or 'go back to your country' so I don't like the younger local people here.*'

Daryl: '*I have had the same experience*'.

Stephan: '*The thing I like least about Hastings is just the security because here I have come to know a few students and about half the*' *students were mugged while they have been here.'*

Michaela: *'I have had a lot of good experiences in Hastings but for me it's not safe here. Some people have very strong prejudices to foreigners.'*

Generally, the students were appreciative of the 'peaceful' surroundings Hastings has to offer and but still referred back to the problem of being antagonized by the local young people. When questioned on whether they would return to Hastings in future many said no. However, I feel it is dangerous to put too much credence on the finding of such enquiries as the individuals and groups questioned, especially teenagers, may be tempted to play to the gallery! My own experience has been that the students who visited with my daughter's organisation made repeated visits to Hastings, year after year, one coming for four consecutive years and another for eight.

Effect of Students on the Local Economy.

In Naomi Gott's survey one local resident is noted as commenting:

'Given Hastings' relative economic backwardness within the context of South East England, the money students bring to many host families, the taxi services, local transport, cafes, pubs, clubs is extremely important; it provides an effective widespread increase to local incomes. Much of the money is spent locally.'

Taking a more jaundiced view were those who accepted that while some businesses did profit from students being in Hastings, they believed that the students shop-lifted, gained from cheaper block bookings, and that host families received poor payment.

Currently, the average student brings about one thousand pounds each into the local economy. The greater part of this sum is for language tuition and extra-curricular activities, e.g.; sports, excursions and social events. The student has between £100 to £250 pocket money, according to the financial position of their family; the student usually spends this money in Hastings, on treats for themselves and gifts to take home to relatives and friends. The matter of payments to host families is a sore subject. The payment is usually in the region of £12-£13 per night (in 2006). It cannot be said that the by-the-hour rate for the job matches the effort put into it, except in the case of the most unprincipled host families. It does however give to mothers with small children or those who find it difficult to get employment for other reasons, an opportunity to earn a small, temporary income. However, these days the hostess is just as likely to have a part or full time job as well. But student hosting is not 'easy money', as the following comment bears out.

Language School Host Family Co-coordinator.

'Some people get the wrong idea and think that hosting students is an easy way to make money and it's not, it's quite hard. You've got people in your house almost all of the time, in your space, and unless you like that and you're a very gregarious person it's going to be really hard. You've got to be there to cook meals, you can't just flit off and so on.'

Hastings perceptions of nuisance value of students.

Throughout the survey there are references to the public transport problems created by students. It is an unfortunate fact that just as the town's working population is setting out, the bulk of the summer students are on their way to school. Language schools have been asked to stagger their start time for lessons, which may help to a degree but certainly not with the vexed subject of students not queuing for buses. Both problems arise again at the end of the day, when students are returning to their host families from leisure activities and the workers are also going home.

The students are not only told by their organisers about the custom of queuing in Britain but they are given booklets that emphasise it as one of the national public behaviours they should observe - but they don't and each year a new intake of students has to be told about this orderly, British habit. On the question of public noise; a telling off from the right person can work quite well. I once witnessed an elderly lady rise from her seat during a performance of The Importance of Being Earnest at Hastings Stables Theatre and boom, 'BE SILENT!' in Lady Bracknellain tones, to a group of noisy, Italian students, to the consternation of her companions and the delight of the rest of the audience, who enjoyed peace henceforth. Opinion seemed to be divided on the matter of how much litter students cause but as our own residents do not always observe the litter laws it would be unfair to blame just students for this.

Effect on local economy.

There is a variety of opinions from families on the subject of whether they make money from hosting students. Some say that one student adds nothing to the family exchequer, other than perhaps better food for the duration of the visit. There is a theory that if two students are hosted then the one pays for the other and there is a profit. But this does not take into account the extra work created for the host mother. When the number of students hosted at one time rises the same applies. It is not until the student number reaches boarding house levels, which I understand is officially six, that a worthwhile profit is possible and this explains the overcrowding some students complain of.

A few families say that as a result of hosting students they can afford to pay for modest home improvements or new household appliances. More obvious are the effects on the local economy: All that extra food and other necessities for students, the wages of English teachers and the schools' administration staff, the money spent by students on entertainments, outings, transport and gifts, amounts to the millions of pounds annual addition to the local economy so often quoted in official statistics.

CHAPTER SIX

COLUMBUS TO THE RESCUE

When I began this book I approached the Hastings Police press office to ask if the force would like to have an involvement with the chapter dealing with crime against students and the efforts of the police, via their specifically targeted Operation Columbus, to prevent these offences. I was referred to a police officer who sounded quite interested when I described the work as a 'public relations opportunity'. After a reasonable interval, during which I heard no more, I approached her again and she said that she had referred my request to an officer more closely involved with Operation Columbus. Again, some weeks passed, until one Sunday morning I received a phone call from this officer, saying that he would try to find time to put something together for me. When there was no further response I started to rationalize the situation and asked myself: 'How is a police officer better employed; in policing or helping a local writer with research? And are we not always hearing how the police are bogged down with paperwork? Should I be giving a police officer cause to do yet more paperwork, in service of a project which neither prevented nor solved crime?' So I turned to the Hastings and St Leonards Observer archive and other sources to provide a picture of the success of Operation Columbus. Operation Columbus was re-launched in April 2001, with an encouraging announcement about the outcome of a court case dealing with offences committed against students.

Hastings Borough Council Press Release

'A Hastings woman who targeted overseas students was sentenced in April to four years imprisonment. The woman - dubbed 'girl ringleader of student - bashers' by the local press - was sentenced at Lewes Crown Court. She pleaded guilty to five counts of robbery on *students last summer after unique work by Hastings police. As the victims had returned to their homes in Germany, police arranged with the British Embassy in Berlin to travel to Germany and show them a videoed identification parade. Robinson was identified by students from the video. This was the first time for Sussex Police that a video identification has been tried in another country. The girl ringleader was charged last August with four robberies and an attempted robbery. She was given three and a half years for the offences and another six months for breaking an earlier 12 month conditional discharge. Recorder David Howker said he hoped the sentence would deter others from robbing students. DC Jon Stainsby, who led the investigation, said: The end result was a direct reflection of the effort from the whole Columbus team. If those that target students think we won't pursue cases because the victims have gone home, they should think again. We hope this sentence sends out a message to them that targeting students will be dealt with very seriously.'*

In a further move to protect overseas students the Streets Ahead project was set up in the summer of 2002 by the Hastings and Rother Youth Development Service, as a pilot scheme to tackle crime against visiting foreign language students in Hastings. Streets Ahead was designed to address tensions between visiting language students and local young people, as well as the growing perception of the town as an unsafe and violent place to visit.   By employing youth workers from European countries such as Germany, Sweden and Finland, the project was able to create a team that had the language skills necessary to communicate with young people in their first language. The youth workers wore red jackets and toured the area in a silver transit van.

Additionally, workshops were run in secondary schools and police identified 'hot spots', which specifically targeted young people who had either offended or displayed behaviour likely to compromise the safety of others. Organisations involved in this project implementation included Sussex Police, Hastings Borough Council, the Youth Service and local educational establishments.

In its first year, the project saw area crime decrease considerably; falling from 170 reported incidents in 2001, to 70 in 2002. Along with this, the town centre was designated a safe haven for foreign students, when the Safe Student Zone campaign was launched in Hastings. Stickers bearing the distinctive Safe Student Zone logo went up in numerous shops in the shopping centre and precinct. Any shops displaying the stickers agreed to act as a safe port of call for foreign students who felt in danger or worried for their safety. A Shopwatch group ran the scheme with a view to liaising with town centre shops to monitor how effectively the Safe Student Zone was running. Inspector Neil Honnor, of Sussex Police, said:

'Safe Student zones are an excellent addition to the already highly successful Operation Columbus scheme. Actual assaults on visiting students have become a rare exception and what the zones offer is reassurance for students who feel threatened. It is an excellent example of Hastings businesses working in partnership to welcome and support these important young visitors to our town.'

The following two reports are reminders, one that overseas students are not entirely blameless when it comes to crime and the other that not all local teenagers are 'student-bashers'.

FISHERMEN NET VANDAL STUDENTS April 2002

'Fishermen caught foreign students red-handed as they went on a wild wrecking spree on boats on the Old Town beach. As the French teenagers hurled rocks at boats and winch shed windows, shards of glass showered over equipment and clothing on board the boats. But the fishermen used their cars to block the students' coach from leaving and tracked down the Eastbourne language school they were heading for.

Now the young vandals have been forced to pay compensation for the damage out of their own pockets. The coach-load of some 40 French students from Paris was on a stop-off at The Stade, en route to an English language school at Eastbourne when the trouble happened. The young teenagers ran onto the beach and hurled stones at boats, smashing wheelhouse and winch shed windows. It was the latest incident of the vandalism which has plagued fishermen and caused thousands of pounds worth of damage to their boats and equipment. It has resulted in fishermen demanding more police and more CCTV. Offences at The Stade over Easter included joyriders in stolen cars using Rock-a-Nore car park as a race track, attempted arson at Underwater World, and kids who jump-started a tractor and tried to push a fishing boat out to sea. Paul Joy, chairman of the Hastings Fishermen's Protection Society, talking about last Monday's damage, said: "One of the fishermen was on the beach and heard the smashing of the windows. The group of students came up by the boats and went to pick up rocks. Mr Joy said the fisherman rang him so he and Graham Coglan parked in front of the students' coach to stop it being driven off. Mr Joy said that he took one of the teachers to his shed to see his own video camera film which showed students climbing on the fishing boat and causing damage. Mr Joy said, "They put ladders up to the boat and climbed on to it, they went down the beach throwing stones at the other boats and breaking two windows on my boat and on a winch shed window as well. It was damage of at least £165. The students had made a determined effort to smash the glass, making three holes in it. Shards of glass were all over the electronics in the boat and in sea boots, clothing and wet weather gear - it's aggravating to say the least." Mr Joy said that they were given the address of the college. "We went over to see them and they gave us a written apology and paid us for the damage and claimed the money back from the 17 to 18-year-olds responsible." The principal was very understanding and told the students the consequences and the danger to the fishermen. The principal took the offences very seriously and agreed to pay the cost of the damage. The offending students also sent letters of apology to the fishermen. Mr Joy said that they were asked by the school if it would be the end of it if they paid compensation, so he was not revealing the name of the school. He added: "It's not local students who seem to be the problem. It's the students in transit who stop to stretch their legs and then get back on the coaches and are gone."

TEENAGER FOILS "STUDENT-BASHERS" 18th June 2002

'A teenager chased two youths who attacked a Venezuelan student in Castle Hill Road. The 16-year-old saw one teenager punch the Spanish-speaking youngster in the face before grabbing his bag. They *then walked off. But the English lad ran after the two youths causing them to drop the ruck-sack before they escaped. Police are now appealing for anyone who saw the incident at 6.30pm last Tuesday (June 11) to come forward. PC Mick Groombridge, who is heading Operation Columbus to target people attacking students, said: "We were impressed by the youngster who chased the attackers. There were adults about who didn't see anything but there must be someone who knows the boys. But despite the incident, PC Groombridge is pleased with the Operation's success. He said: "It has been quiet and seems the language schools have been passing on good advice. More students are travelling in groups but this Castle Hill Road area is becoming a trouble-spot which we are now targeting. Street Wardens are patrolling similar areas and we welcome their help.'*

STUDENT ROBBED AT KNIFEPOINT 21st August 2002

'A slightly built 14-year-old Italian language student broke down in tears as he told police how he was robbed at knifepoint. The youth was with a 15-year-old fellow Italian student when they were robbed in Bulverhythe Road on Friday night. PC Andy Simpson said that in the Bulverhythe Road incident: "One of them was only a small 14 year-old and he reckoned the knife was held to his throat. They had left the disco on the front and walked back home to Bexhill Road. The robber pushed them both into Bulverhythe Road and took everything they had on them. The attacker got away with both their bags and contents. One bag, a Puma, contained portable CD player, certificates from school and a wallet containing 50 Euros and £5. The total value was £200. The other, which was a plain bag, had a Panasonic portable CD player and 50 Euros. It was valued at £160. Both students returned to their home country at the weekend.'

CZECH STUDENTS ATTACKED 25th May 2003

'Six teenage students were robbed in three violent early evening attacks while staying in the town. In two of the incidents the victims were threatened and robbed at knifepoint and in the other the students were punched, kicked and pulled to the ground. The start of the summer has brought with it the problem of foreign student attacks.

Under Operation Columbus, police officers are investigating crimes against a number of visitors to the town's language schools and are trying to get the message to students to be aware of safety issues. In the latest series of attacks none of the victims needed hospital treatment but they were left shaken and upset. The first attack happened on Tuesday May 20 at 6.25pm when three Czech students were walking in Quantock Drive and Mendip Gardens. A young man and two young women grabbed two of the students' rucksacks and tried to pull them off their shoulders. Two more street robberies took place at 5pm on Wednesday 21st May. A young Czech student was threatened with a knife by a man in Old London Road and had his cash and Nokia mobile phone stolen. At the same time two young German students were robbed at knifepoint in Cromer Walk in the Blacklands area. The robber got away with his victims' money. Chief Inspector Ken Taylor said: "We want to encourage these young people to come to the town but they are quite vulnerable because of their youth and they do not know the area. Operation Columbus is about providing advice and guidance to students through language schools and host families, and proactive policing and investigation. We have already arrested one person for theft from a student and other suspects are being identified." Chief Inspector Taylor said that Columbus officers are starting to identify hot spots of offences where police and street wardens need to be more visible. "Students need to know all routes to and from their host family's house and make sure they follow those that are well-lit. We do not want them to walk around absolutely petrified as it is only a small number of students who are victims of crime but I would urge them to be more aware. We need victims to report incidents so we can find out where we are needed to be more visible and to look at long-term solutions."

YOUTHS JAILED FOR 14 YEARS FOR FOREIGN STUDENT ROBBERIES 25th June 2004

'Three youths have been jailed for a series of terrifying knifepoint robberies. The three 18 year old youths were sentenced to a total of 14 years after appearing at Lewes Crown Court last Friday. The trio was arrested by police after committing four robberies within half an hour on June 23 last year. Police claim the sentences confirm the success of

Operation Columbus, set up in the late 1990s to combat a plague of assaults on foreign visitors to the town. A police spokesman said: "Let this be a warning to others who target foreign students. Hastings police will vigorously pursue them and they are likely to end up with a custodial sentence." The attacks began in Mount Pleasant Crescent at around 11.30pm. An English youth aged about 14 was accosted by the gang whilst returning home from an evening out. The youth was threatened with a knife, whilst the gang went through his pockets before making off with a CD player and a baseball cap. Barely 15 minutes later the gang brandished a knife at two teenage Japanese students returning to their language school. The students, a boy and girl, were robbed of cash and a mobile phone whilst walking on Laton Road. The third incident occurred at midnight, when a Russian student in his late teens was robbed of cash on the same road. The student tried to fight off his attackers after they held a knife to his throat, but he was wrestled to the ground. None of the victims were injured in the attacks. The trio was in custody at Hastings police station within half an hour of the final attack, after uniformed police officers cornered them outside Safeways, in Queens Road. The items reported stolen were found in their possession, although not all the money was recovered. Police arranged for the victims to identify the robbers before the foreign students returned home, and Sussex Police paid for the two Japanese students to fly back for the court hearing. Two of the offenders pleaded guilty to four robberies and were each sentenced to four years in a young offenders' detention centre. The third denied the charges but was found guilty by a jury on June 10 and sentenced to six years in a detention centre on 18th June. Police report assaults on foreign students are down this year, with 24 incidents occurring and nine arrests made since 1st April 2004. Operation Columbus is designed to tackle attacks on foreign students, which numbered 158 over the summer period in 2000, through increased summer patrols and fortnightly meetings with language schools and council representatives. Speaking after the case, DS Mike Ashcroft said: "These were nasty robberies mainly involving foreign visitors to Hastings. Attacks on foreign students are treated with the utmost seriousness under the police's Operation Columbus and these sentences demonstrate that the court will not tolerate them."'

Promotional 'Student Safety' feature published in the Hastings and St Leonards Observer June 30th 2006

'Operation Columbus is now up and running for 2006 across the East Sussex Division and will continue throughout the summer into early autumn. The operation which is run every year aims to provide a safe environment for visiting international students. Inspector Gary Keating overseeing the operation within East Sussex said, 'Foreign students are vital for the area's tourist industry and we want them to be safe - and feel safe - when they visit us. We want them to enjoy their stay and the facilities available and go home with only good memories.' The hard-hitting message from East Sussex Division is, 'Target a student and we will target you'. Police action as part of Operation Columbus will feature high visibility policing in hot spot areas, specially trained investigators to deal with incidents involving students, dedicated patrols, plain clothes surveillance and use of CCTV. Host families are asked to play their part by passing on good advice to their students, such as not to walk home alone at night, only take essentials when going out and do not carry unnecessary cash or valuables. Inspector Gary Keating says, 'We have made comprehensive preparations in order to welcome international visitors. We will work closely with our local Crime and Disorder Reduction partnerships across the division, along with language schools, student bodies and local authorities to ensure that our visitors have an enjoyable and pleasant visit'. Letters explaining all about Operation Columbus and the police activity involved are being sent to people previously convicted of or suspected of being involved in incidents against language students. Gary added: 'We have already identified individuals who are known to target foreign students and are in the process of making them fully aware of the our intentions to crack down on any such incidents this year. We will pay particular attention to individuals with such a history or who may have on-going intentions to commit criminal activity against this vulnerable group. Many of the students are vulnerable because of their age, lack of understanding of English or knowledge of English law. It is important that they recognise that we take their safety seriously.'

Sussex Police provides crime prevention advice and materials to language schools including videos and leaflets about English law and what to do in the event of a crime. All the materials are available in different languages, which include crime reporting forms. Further crime prevention advice and information on Operation Columbus can be found on the Sussex Police website. Operation Columbus is a force-wide initiative and is a partnership between police, language schools, student bodies and the local authorities. Central to Operation Columbus is a manual which provides partnership agencies with a wide range of practices and tactics they can apply to ensure that students have a safe time during their visit. Statistics relating to reported incidents of attacks on students are; 2004- 3, 2005- 20, 2006 - June 2006- 8'.

An additional statement - from either Hastings Overseas Students Advisory Council or Hastings Tourism Department:

'Language students are a major factor in the Hastings and St Leonards visitor economy. We have 25 registered language schools in the town and we welcome around 35,000 language students every year who contribute around £35 million to the local economy. As well as the many French and German students we have welcomed for years we are seeing a rise in the number of Scandinavian students after that market declined considerably. The number of Eastern European students has also increased significantly in recent years and there has been a rise in South American students and those from other developing countries. Many of these are more mature students, in their twenties or older who come for several weeks on intensive courses.'

ASHAMED OF THE TOWN THEY LOVED. 28th July 2006

'Spineless yobs are picking on foreign students in a sickening campaign of hatred. Teenagers from overseas, who provide a huge boost to the town's economy, are regularly the victims of unprovoked verbal and physical assaults. Police say the number of attacks on foreign students is in decline - but the Observer has learned many incidents go unreported. Twin sisters, local girls who spent their summer holidays working with students at STS Language School, say *the behaviour of a minority is blighting the image of Hastings. They took a group of foreign students to Alexandra Park on Wednesday last week to play cricket and they were soon set upon by groups of thugs. One twin said: "As soon as we got there, one of the 15-year-old Swedish boys was attacked by eight or nine youths in their late teens. They shouted abuse at him and one of them slapped him around the head. One of the others hit him with an ice cream tub. We called the police and the youths left, so we carried on playing cricket. Then, about half and hour later, another group came over and surrounded me, calling me all names under the sun. "They called me an f******g French frog and other much worse things, and threatened to attack me. One of them kept saying, 'I'm going to dash you', whatever that means, and told me to hand over my mobile phone. It makes me feel ashamed to say I come from Hastings. This xenophobic minority is the loudest group out there, and they're giving the town a bad name. I feel betrayed and let down by the community I grew up in. Every year students bring money and custom to Hastings, and all these yobs bring is notoriety." The local girl's sister had similar problems at Alexandra Park last Wednesday when a group of youths called her 'a traitor to England' and spat in her face. They also stole a bag belonging to one of the Italian students in her care. The girl said: "When I was growing up here, I didn't realise there was such a problem in Hastings. I thought the community was tolerant, diverse and forward-thinking. But working with foreign students over the summer has shown me there is a nasty, racist core of people here who are doing the town no favours at all." A spokesman for the police said the number of reported assaults on foreign students is down this year, compared to previous years.'*

Operation Columbus Personal Safety Guide for International Students

The public is often critical of the apparent failure of schools or the police to inform and educate overseas students about their personal safety and how to conform to the customs and behaviour in the UK. This criticism is unfair as every effort is made to deal with this situation.

The police provide a wide range of advice and guidance for students, to be distributed by local authorities and language schools. This can be sent to schools either on request or through Police Officers/Staff linking into Operation Columbus. Language schools should appoint staff as liaison officers to ensure good communications between students, schools, councils and police which help prevent problems and also deal with any that occur.

Settling In.

Obviously when you arrive in a different country it can be confusing.

You will have to rely on your host family, your language school or college. Do not be frightened to ask both; they are there to help you.

Read all the literature you have been given and keep all your student safety leaflets with you at all times. Find out the location of the venues you have to visit and the details of how to get there. Try not to travel alone. This is always a good rule to follow. Whenever possible travel with others but only if you know who they are and if you can trust them.

Before undertaking any journey you should: Think ahead, be prepared, be aware and avoid risks, never assume.

Staying safe on the street or campus.

At times everyone feels worried about becoming a victim of crime when they are in public places. By taking a few simple precautions you can help yourself stay safe.

Be Strong. Walk confidently and with purpose. Hold your head up and look as if you know where you are going.

Safety in Numbers. Go around with friends, especially in high risk or dark areas. Avoid wearing clothes or carrying possessions that will identify you as a student. Stick to well-lit busy routes; avoid short cuts across waste ground or wooded areas.

Stay Alert. Be aware of what is going on around you. If you're listening to a personal stereo you won't hear what is going on.

Consider carrying a personal attack alarm. Remember it is an offence to carry in the street a self-defence spray (CS Gas) or any other weapon, such as flick knives or blades.

Staying safe on the move.

By remembering a few general points when travelling on public transport you can help yourself to be safe and feel safe.

Plan your route. Check on buses and train times before you leave. Always stay in well lit areas on platforms, near to a telephone if there is one.

Remember to queue for buses and services. It is polite and prevents the pavements from being obstructed.

On trains or the tube try to sit in a carriage that is near the driver or guard or sit near other passengers. If you feel uncomfortable about anybody in your carriage move to a different compartment.

Make sure you know where the alarm or emergency cord is. Use it if necessary.

Tell a member of the transport staff if you see anything suspicious.

By Taxicab.

Have the number of a reputable taxicab firm ready for whenever you may need one.

Always sit in the back and only share taxicabs with people you know; it's safer and cheaper.

If you chat with the driver do not disclose your personal details.

Ensure you have your fare ready before arriving at your destination.

By Bus.

Avoid isolated bus stops.

Check the timetables before travelling.

Always sit on the lower deck.

Remember the driver can help you if you need assistance - press the bell in an emergency.

Rail Safety.

Never walk across or touch railway lines - they can kill you.

Do not open train doors until the train has completely stopped and NEVER open the door on the side opposite to the platform.

Avoid Conflict Situations.

It is wise to know a few things about taking care of yourself and how to avoid getting into dangerous situations.

Never assume it won't happen to you. Trust your intuition, act positively.

Your aim should be to move away; meeting aggression with aggression leads to confrontation and you could get hurt.

Don't get drawn into arguments, don't get involved, walk away from the situation. You might have to bite your tongue but that is better than getting bitten!

Drunken people will NOT listen to reason, walk away from them

If you are attacked your safely is paramount. Shout and scream, run away if you can. The law allows you to use reasonable force to defend yourself. If someone comes at you with a weapon you can use anything that comes to hand to defend yourself. However you are NOT allowed to carry a weapon in a public place, even for self defence. If you think you are being threatened go to a shop or well-lit house and do not be afraid to ask for help. Ask somebody to call the police.

Talk about it

End the silence. If you have been involved in an attack or have been threatened or bullied don't keep it to yourself. Tell a friend or someone you trust. Your host family, language school representatives or local police will all be able to offer help and guidance with these matters.

Don't blame yourself. The problem is not you. By talking to someone you can beat it and put it behind you.

It is also recognised that students can either intentionally or unwittingly create problems themselves. In some cases this can be due to not understanding local customs or laws. To help overcome this problem a range of colour posters featuring the cartoon character 'Columbus' aim to advise students on daily life in Britain.

Your behaviour

It is usual to join the back of a queue in Britain - don't push in, it will make people angry.

Do not walk straight into the road - remember to look right when you cross the road - cars in England drive on the left.

Laws in England may be different from your home country. This especially applies to tobacco, alcohol and self defence sprays. You must not carry drugs with you of any kind (unless prescribed by a doctor), or use any illegal drugs including LSD or amphetamines. You must be 16 to buy and smoke cigarettes or tobacco.

Don't drop litter - put it in the bin or take it home with you.

Be quiet on your way home at night. Don't block paths - if you need to group together, find an area with plenty of space.

You must be 18 to buy alcohol - most English pubs don't welcome under 18's.

Don't steal - you will be arrested and probably sent home.

Never carry all of your money or passport with you and try to carry your valuables such as cameras out of view.

GROUP PROFILES

In 1999 John Dunstar, the principal of Eastbourne Language and Activity Centre, Eastbourne, drew up a list of personal safety guidelines for overseas students and also nationality group profiles in order to assist the police with their recently launched Operation Columbus, an initiative to prevent crime against students. This was run as a pilot in Eastbourne and is now adopted by all constabularies in regions that host overseas students. John Dunstar said that the Eastbourne police had used his group profiles to help them better understand the behaviour of non-nationals, either as victims or perpetrators of crime.

The profiles are intended as a guide to the behaviour and reactions of young people between the ages of 13-18 years. John Dunstar said that they comprise a number of comments made about the country, life and normal behaviour in those countries and how this translates into patterns of behaviour while in the UK. He emphasises that they are subjective comments and based on nothing but experience gained from working with young people from these countries over the past 25 years. There is no empirical or statistical study underpinning the comments.

Many of the comments hold good for adults but they are based on a social knowledge of the background of young people, how they behave and what they do in their own countries. For many, this can be quite different from what happens in the UK. The profiles are by their very nature generalisations. There are always exceptions and clearly the subjective assessment by individual police officers in the middle of an incident must prevail. However some of the comments might help in making that subjective assessment accurate, thereby easing what is always a difficult job.

In the accounts of host families who have contributed their recollections to Host Families Wanted, it can be seen that some of the national characteristics noted by the families are also highlighted in John Dunstar's lists, particularly the observations made by Kay Green, who was both a student hostess and an EFL teacher. John did not include a list for Middle Eastern Countries, possibly because 16 years ago fewer students visited the UK from this region. Also excluded are the Eastern Europeans, who did not begin to appear at language schools in high numbers until the mid-1990s. The references to smoking are also interestingly out of date, demonstrating how the message about the dangers of smoking has proliferated world wide.

John Dunstar said that it would be singularly inappropriate for him to try to identify crime by nationality and the profiles make no attempt to do so. A shoplifter is a shoplifter, no matter where the offender comes from and all nationalities have them. The profiles are simply general character summaries derived from his own experience of having worked with overseas students and travelled extensively in their countries.

Spanish, Italian and the Latin Countries of the Mediterranean.

Comments on society and life in the above countries.

* They have an outdoor society; they frequently go out and stay out late. This is especially so for the Spanish.

* They have little experience of community policing.

* The family unit is of great importance.

* They can often react emotionally.

* They are extremely tactile. They will embrace and touch.

* Their personal space requirement is small.

* It is easy to acquire alcohol when young.

* Smoking is still widespread. There is less awareness of the harmful effects of smoking.

* Congregating in groups on the streets is widespread and does not indicate antisocial or threatening behaviour.

* Their society is socially disciplined but at the same time laid back and relaxed.

* The level of petty crime in cities is high. However, in the provinces it tends to be lower than in the UK.

Patterns of behaviour in the UK

* They are quite confident and not afraid to use their English language even though at times this lacks accuracy. They communicate fairly well.

* They are very sociable people and mix easily.

* They like to go out frequently in the evenings; they find it difficult to come to terms with returning home by 11.00pm to conform to UK behaviour patterns. They find it hard to understand that people on

English streets after midnight are often 'undesirables'.

* They are streetwise, reflecting the level of petty crime in their own countries.

* They are largely fearful of authority and most would be very nervous if confronted or challenged by a police officer. In extreme cases they would react emotionally or even panic.

* They are extremely gregarious. They frequently congregate in large groups on the street and these groups can become very noisy, as they are in their own country. They will be completely unaware that this can be interpreted differently in the UK or that in certain circumstances it could be considered antisocial.

* They are highly vociferous and excitable but this hardly ever translates into physical aggression. They are verbally confrontational; they will argue in a highly animated fashion that can be quite intimidating to an outsider.

* Physical confrontation is extremely rare. Thy can be provocative verbally but will invariably retreat from physical situations, unless acting in self-defence.

* Emotional reactions can be somewhat extreme especially in emergency situations or at times of distress.

* They are unlikely to abuse alcohol as they are used to it. Drunken behaviour is rare, especially in the case of the Spanish.

Northern and Central Europeans - Germany, Austria Switzerland, etc.

Comments on the society and life in the above countries.

* It is not an outdoor society; it is very similar to our own.

* Germanic based languages are very direct, often loud and can appear aggressive.

* They have very little experience of community policing.

* They are less tactile than the Latin people but probably more so than the British.

* Their personal space requirement is similar to the British.

* It is quite easy to acquire alcohol when young; alcohol abuse among young people is a problem in some inner city areas.

* Smoking is still widespread; there is less awareness of the harmful effects of smoking.

* Their society is socially disciplined.

* The level of petty crime is similar to the UK in both cities and provinces. However, the level of petty crime in the alpine regions of Austria and Switzerland is low.

Patterns of Behaviour in the UK.

* They are usually confident and are not afraid to use their English language even thought at times this lacks accuracy. They communicate well.

* German translates very directly and does not possess the same politeness strategies as English. As a result, the language expressed can often sound very rude and aggressive when neither was intended. However, impertinence and insolence would not be misinterpreted.

* They are quite sociable people and mix well but not as easily as the Latins.

* They like to go out frequently in the evenings while in the UK. This is not done so much in their own countries so we have to be aware of the 'letting off the leash' situation.

* They are fairly streetwise.

* They are not as fearful of authority as some nationalities but most would be a little nervous and quite respectful if confronted or challenged by a police officer but they are unlikely to panic in such a situation.

* They are generally not gregarious like Latins but they do congregate in groups in the street in the UK and will be unaware of the social consequences. As they are not used to doing this in their own countries this can lead to group confidence and out-of-character behaviour
.

* They are not afraid of confrontation. Violence however is rare, other than in self-defence. Alcohol abuse can be a problem at times.

Japanese

Comments on society and life of the above

* This is not an outdoor society.

* The family unit very strong.

* Society is highly disciplined and male dominated. People usually conform through a strong sense of self-discipline.

* Japanese people are naturally quiet and reserved until you gain their confidence. Their society teaches them that it is rude to put yourself forward too much. Consequently translations of words such as extrovert or outgoing will hold negative connotation and will not be complimentary to the Japanese.

* English is taught from a very early age in all schools. However, they concentrate on reading and writing skills and therefore speaking and listening to English is not advanced.

* Very rarely does Japanese culture allow a direct 'no' in reply to a question.

* They have very little experience of community policing.

* Punishment for anti-social or criminal behaviour revolves around public shaming. As a result the level of petty crime is negligible and virtually non-existent in the provinces.

* They live in large urban conurbations but a small town in the provinces of Japan can have in excess of 100,000 inhabitants.

* They are less tactile than Latin people but probably more so than the British.

* Their personal space requirement is very small.

* It is not easy to acquire alcohol when young but its abuse among some young can be a problem in some inner cities.

* Smoking is still widespread; there is less awareness of the harmful effects of smoking.

Patterns of behaviour in the UK

* They are very shy and extremely self-conscious about using their English language. This conceals a normally strong foundation in the grammar and vocabulary of the language.

* They will have difficulty in understanding the spoken language.

* They are initially shy and reserved but are essentially very sociable people and after a preliminary phase will mix quite easily.

* They are quite gregarious and enjoy going out in the evening.

* They are not streetwise and will be unaware of the need to keep a close eye on their possessions while in public places.

* It is a cash society and as a result Japanese students often carry large quantities of cash without being aware of the potential dangers.

* They are extremely respectful of authority and would be very nervous if confronted or challenged by a police officer.

* If they are questioned do not misinterpret silence, they almost certainly will not have understood or be too nervous to reply.

* Also be aware that they may give what appears to be a positive reply when they really mean no or mean to respond negatively.

* If they think they have transgressed in any way, or even if they have not, they will be extremely nervous and terrified of being publicly shamed.

* They are unlikely to abuse alcohol as they follow the rules.

* Drunken behaviour is rare in young people.

This list is not intentionally racist. I wish that I had access to John Dunstar's lists when I began hosting students over 40 years ago; it would have prevented the small misunderstandings that arose in my household from cultural differences.

CHAPTER SEVEN

ACRONYMS AND AGGRAVATIONS

In 1977/78 a number of local language schools set up a forum to discuss student issues. The group called itself Hastings Association of Language School Organisations – HALCO. Unfortunately records of its inception and membership have been lost but some of the founder members were Embassy School, HELC and EF. At that time Hastings Borough Council did not wish to be involved with the project. The purpose of HALCO was to provide a system of mutual support and an opportunity to network about unsuitable host families and other issues and to increase student security. It was HALCO who drew up the original Language School Voluntary Code of Practice that is still in use today by the Hastings Overseas Student Advisory Council, the code remaining almost unchanged from its HALCO form. It was a very enterprising American lady employed in the Hastings Borough Council Tourism and Marketing Department who suggested that HALCO should be invited to work with the local authority.

A Hastings Student Liaison Working Party was formed by Hastings Borough Council in 1991 and in 1994 a partnership was formed with the town's language schools, representatives of the police, public transport, the health authorities and local authority tourist attractions. All the local language schools were invited to a pilot meeting at Hastings Town Hall in the spring of 1995. I attended this meeting; there was such a throng of representatives from the schools that extra seating was brought in and late comers found standing room only. Before formal introductions were made, the guests stood about in groups, discreetly speculating as to who was who, while exchanging conventional shop talk about the forthcoming season, mostly on the topic of student numbers and the current preoccupation with street violence against students.

Hastings Borough Council put forward the HALCO Voluntary Code of Practice for language schools, explaining that if a school agreed to abide by this code they would have the right to display the HOSAC logo on their documentation and its certificate at their premises. Some weeks later, on April 25th 1995, all those who had signed up and paid up were invited to a reception for the presentation of the certificates at the town hall. My colleagues from Italy were on a business visit to Hastings at the time and it was my daughter's task to receive the mayor's handshake and the A4 card that declared our organisation a HOSAC member. There was the standard local press group photo of the mayor and the new certificate holders, squashed together on the marble staircase of the town hall. The evening concluded with refreshments; I felt a twinge of citizen-guilt at the expenditure of council tax money on the posh nibbles and wine - the delicious and appropriately named 1066, from local vineyard, Carr Taylor. This hospitality was repeated at a few subsequent meetings, gradually declining in generosity over the seasons, until it was reduced to a cup of coffee. I felt an easing of my guilt; forgetting that there was an annual fee for HOSAC certification.

For several years I attended every meeting of HOSAC; the main assemblies were held in April and October, with subsidiary meetings between times to discuss specific issues. As I wore every hat in our organisation I seemed to attend most of these but I always found the meetings devoted to student accommodation the most helpful, offering an informal opportunity to exchange information, particularly about rogue host families. At the bi-annual meetings of HOSAC representatives of bodies associated with the welfare or leisure of the students were frequently present. Hastings Police, the local bus company boss and managers of Hastings Borough Council's sports facilities addressed the members and answered questions on the concerns that arose in their particular fields. I have never been a very keen believer in the committee set-up as a way of getting things done and I think it can sometimes be a misuse of resources. This belief was reinforced one evening when I attended a HOSAC meeting at Hastings Town Hall. As I crossed the town centre, a fracas started between five or six kicking and punching young men outside the McDonald's outlet at Wellington Place. The solitary young policeman on duty ran full pelt to intervene. When I reached the meeting there were five representatives of the police force sitting on the question panel. They were a young woman and four older male officers, probably none of them capable of dealing single-handedly with a public brawl but it highlighted the ill-balanced nature of policing these days. The officers on the panel made a number of points and proposals and the language school staff present listened politely and asked sensible questions, sadly conscious that most of the problems especially that of crime against students would continue. One of the madder ideas mooted at a HOSAC meeting, (in fairness to our local police force, I should say that I think this came from outside our constabulary), was that young adult student leaders should patrol the violence hot-spots in the town at night in specially marked T-shirts, to act as security escorts to overseas students. (The word 'target' springs to mind). In effect, to be unpaid, untrained assistants to the police. One school owner said that this was the time she stopped going to HOSAC. In a lighter mood: At another meeting a suggestion was put forward by a HBC representative that each school should award a prize to their best host family. The accommodation officers looked aghast! Their host families, like babies in a beauty contest, are each and every one of them, 'the best.'

A founder member of HALCO told me that the organisation joined with HBC in the belief that it would help to get practical things done, like shelters at Sea Road, to give cover to the hundreds of students who arrived there in coaches. She said that instead, in her opinion, HOSAC clouded the essential issues by bringing in outside bodies, becoming too bureaucratic and diluting the original aims of HALCO. She conceded that the shelters were installed after some years, but only two small models, completely inadequate for the huge influx of students. It caused some wry amusement that the open sides of these shelters faced the sea, only few yards away, and also the direction from which came the most rainfall. Another success for HOSAC was to get a public telephone installed at Falaise Road, a prime picking up and setting down spot for students. Probably one of HOSAC's most worthwhile acts was in identifying language schools that fell below the accepted standard by using unsuitable buildings for teaching and overcrowding the classrooms, issues that could be tackled under the local authority health and safety regulations and thus bring about closure of the school. There were also rumours of an organisation that walked its newly arrived students up and down a street, knocking on doors to ask, 'Would you like to board a student?' This may be an urban myth but several people I interviewed had heard about it.

In 1999, in a move that proved to be successful, Hastings Borough Council, in partnership with ITS English School, offered local residents the chance to learn to teach English to overseas students. A bursary to cover the fees, funded by Hastings Borough Council, gave local unemployed residents, men and women with dependants and people with disabilities the opportunity to join the course and gain a TESOL qualification to teach English as a foreign language. The qualification to be completed before the 2000 intake of foreign students. This initiative was supported by HOSAC as part of their efforts to pursue excellent standards, and to enhance Hastings & St Leonards reputation as a premier destination for learning English. The course was to take place on two evenings a week and the occasional Saturday. To qualify for a grant applicants must have lived in Hastings & St Leonards for at least 12 months, be in receipt of unemployment benefit, family credit or disability benefit and be prepared to teach locally for at least one season. The director of ITS said that the scheme was devised to encourage local people to take the first step in qualifying for teaching EFL and to learn about teaching methods. Those not eligible for a bursary were still able to join the course but would be be liable for the course fee. Many successful participants in the courses went on to successful EFL careers, at home and abroad.

This copy of the HOSAC Voluntary Code of Practice, was copied from the Hastings Borough Council website in 2006. The following transcription of the code remains true to the original text, except in some cases of punctuation. It is not intended to replace the original Code, a copy of which is available from HBC. The Code has a number of sub-clauses which make for repetitious reading, so these are summarized in some instances.

VOLUNTARY CODE OF PRACTICE

For the purposes of this Declaration the word school is used to mean a school or Summer Course Organisation for the teaching of English as a foreign language.

The Code of Practice was produced as the result of discussions between English Language Schools and English Language Summer

Course Organisations operating in Hastings and other organisations concerned with the functioning of schools or affected by them. It was produced in an attempt to ensure that schools and course organisations operate in a responsible manner towards their students, maintain good relations with Hastings' permanent residents as well as with visitors and enhance the resort's reputation as a centre for learning.

All schools operating in Hastings are asked to endorse the Code of Practice, which consists of this Introductory Statement and a detailed Declaration containing the standards of operation, which is attached. Adherence to the principles and standards is voluntary and is separate from any requirements of the British Council and the ARELS/FELCO Group for recognition by those bodies. While the Code of Practice is a voluntary agreement undertaken by language schools and summer course organisations, Hastings Borough Council fully supports the aims of the code. Hastings Borough Council is in no position to enforce the Code and indeed has no legal powers to do so. However, in any approach to the Council and the South East England Tourist Board for information, the importance of the Code in ensuring that acceptable standards are provided will be stressed.

The Code recognises that there is a wide variety of schools offering courses in English as a foreign language operating in the Hastings area. Each school has its own characteristics and needs. It is not intended that the Code should inhibit the freedom and ability of organisations to offer a full range of courses.

In general, all schools adhering to the Code should ensure that their promotional literature and brochures are strictly accurate and informative - and do not give, either in text or illustration, a misleading impression of the services offered or the status of the organisation.

EDUCATION

The Declaration covers the standards of operation required for education, premises, leisure and social activities, student welfare, host family accommodation, transport and local bus services. To ensure that educational standards are maintained at all times all students undertaking a course in Hastings should receive a basic minimum standard of tuition, however short or modest their course. This should ensure that students are not disappointed with their course from a language tuition point of view and that the reputation of Hastings as a centre of learning is not devalued. All schools should strive towards having a director of studies who holds a R.S.A. preparatory certificate or equivalent. The declaration sets out standards of hours of tuition, class size, teacher qualification, course content and student attainment reports.

Summary of Clauses:

The school is expected to undertake that they will provide students with a minimum of 10 hours of supervised tuition per week in classes of not more than 16 students, under the control of one teacher, who is appropriately qualified.

A certificate of attendance and, if required, a progress report will be issued for each student at the end of the course.

PREMISES

Just as the achievement of a good standard of education provision is important it is essential to obtain a satisfactory standard for premises used by schools if a high standard of learning is to be retained. The school asserts that its premises will comply with all necessary fire, environmental health and planning consents and all permanent employees must be fully conversant with current fire procedures.

LEISURE AND SOCIAL ACTIVITIES

One of the most noticeable features of schools to the Hastings resident are the large groups of young people which congregate in the town centre each summer. To ensure any potential conflict between the schools and the residents is kept to a minimum it is desirable for schools to supplement their language teaching activities with a high level of organised leisure and social activity. In particular, a full programme with close supervision is needed for under-eighteens, unless they are accompanied by a parent or other adult. The Declaration includes the need to provide social and leisure events and recreational activities and to avoid overcrowding by students in the town centre. Where possible schools should ensure that host families are aware of their responsibilities in ensuring that their students, particularly if the are under 18, return to host accommodation each evening at the time specified by the school.

STUDENT WELFARE

Students at schools range from young people, some under 16 to mature adults and from those with no knowledge of or experience of life in a foreign country to seasoned travellers. It is important that assistance is given by schools to those with little experience of living away from home. Schools should provide for the welfare of their students, paying particular attention to the needs of the young. To this end schools should appoint a responsible adult specifically to attend to the needs of students and to be always available in case of difficulties. It may be found useful to provide leaflets or give an introductory talk to students, outlining the habits, laws and customs of the British, the sort of behaviour expected in Britain and other useful information. Schools need to accept responsibility for their students, reserving the right to expel or remove students from host families and send them home if appropriate. The Declaration calls for the provision of a responsible adult to supervise student welfare and the issue of identity cards.

STANDARDS OF HOST FAMILY ACCOMMODATION

If students are on their first visit to Britain the standard of accommodation and food and the welcome they receive from their host family or hostel will colour their future regard for Britain and the British. It is therefore important that students are provided with a good minimum standard of accommodation, that schools ensure that this standard is maintained and that the relationship between host and student is a satisfactory one. Schools should ensure that one person is specifically concerned with accommodation and that inspections are carried out and complaints quickly investigated. The school prospectus should state clearly the accommodation arrangements provided or available. The Declaration calls for the provision of an accommodation officer, for the inspection of accommodation and the investigation of complaints, clear prospectus details and controlled allocation of accommodation.

TRANSPORT AND LOCAL BUS SERVICES

This section has been specifically included because of difficulties which have occurred due to the numbers of students using public transport, often at peak hours when congestion is already acute. Whenever possible, schools should stagger tuition hours. The Declaration covers providing information to transport operators, use of season tickets, off-peak travel, consultations and basic road-use instruction.

Summary of Clauses:

In order to minimize the congestion of the resort's transport services the school undertakes to provide bus companies, before the summer, with an indication of its students' likely travel patterns during July and August, specifying:

The likely number of students, areas where they will be lodged, relevant bus routes and the times they are likely to travel by bus.

To encourage students to use the appropriate season or multi-journey bus tickets.

To consult bus companies, when establishing lesson times during the summer, where these are likely to have an effect on local bus use.

To consult British Rail when making arrangements for large groups of students to travel by train, particularly with regard to commuter hours.

To provide some basic instruction in road safety and the Highway Code for students who travel by bicycle instead of by public transport.

COMPLAINTS PROCEDURE.

Schools who sign the Declaration will be issued with an annual certificate for display in their premises. A copy of the Declaration must also be prominently displayed at all times alongside the certificate. Copies of the Declaration must be readily available on request for students and their families, host families or providers of services

116

associated with the industry. It is expected that the majority of complaints or allegations stemming from violation of the Code of Practice can be satisfactorily resolved internally by the school concerned. Complaints that are not satisfactorily resolved can be referred to a small panel of Hasting Language School Organisers and representatives of Hasting Borough Council. Although the panel does not have any legal powers it can exclude any school from displaying the Hastings Code of Practice Certificate and withdraw the right of the use of the logo and/or any other services outlined in the Code of Practice. Where appropriate, serious complaints or allegations will be referred to statutory organisations, such as Trading Standards, the Environmental Health Department, Planning Department, etc.

The schools listed below have signed the Code of Practice, which includes a detailed Declaration outlining operating standards, requiring them to provide appropriate premises, a good standard of education, varied and attractive leisure and social activities (to help avoid large groups of students congregating in the town centre), adequate student welfare facilities, advice on host family accommodation and local transport services. Although voluntary, the Code is fully supported by Hastings Borough Council and only signatories of the Code are promoted in response to requests for information made to the Council and the South East England Tourist Board.

In addition to signing the Code of Practice, a number of schools are British Council and ARELS recognised and have been inspected by the British Council in all areas of their operation including teaching and teacher qualifications. The list was last updated 30th June 2006 but may include schools that have moved premises or are no longer in business.

Language Schools in the Hastings area

Abbey Study Holidays

15 Magpie Close
St Leonards on Sea
East Sussex TN38 8DY
Telephone: 01424 441360
e-Mail: sleakey@toucansurf.com

Director: Mr and Mrs Leakey

Private English lessons only. Prices upon request. Evening and weekend lessons available.

Cambridge Gardens College

6-7 Cambridge Gardens
Hastings
East Sussex TN34 1EH
Telephone: 01424 422322
Fax: 01424 421257
e-Mail: fran@cgc-england.com
Web: www.cgc-england.com.

Cambridge Gardens College is a language centre specialising in linguistic stays for youngsters. Our programmes include junior residential courses (8-13) and teenage home-stay courses (14-18). Course fees are fully inclusive of all tuition, accommodation, sports and cultural activities, local transport, excursions, visits and air fares from any EU country! The maximum class size is 10 students. Cambridge Gardens College maintains close liaison with its host families who are visited and selected by the director personally. Our programmes are offered to both individuals and groups. Our centre operates all year round. Cambridge Gardens College is recognised for quality by L'OFFICE in France.

Charles Eaton College of English Language

Quince House
Battle Road
Three Cups
Heathfield
East Sussex TN21 9LS
Telephone: 01435 831078
Fax: 01435 830188
e-Mail: charleseaton@lineone.net
Web: website.lineone.net/~charleseaton.

Director and Accommodation Officer: Mrs Norma Cooksley

Charles Eaton College is a summer language school that specialises in groups or individual students and provides 1 to 8 week general English courses. All to include full board host family accommodation and excursions to London and other cities. All transfers to and from UK, pick up points for 10 or more and 1 leader free with all groups.

EAC Language School Hastings

43-45 Cambridge Gardens
Hastings
East Sussex TN34 1EN
Telephone: 01424 438025
Fax: 01424 438050
e-Mail: jperkins@eac4english.com
Web: www.eacworld.com.

Director: Jane Perkins
Accommodation Officer: Merryn Watson

Embassy CES

Gensing Manor
Dane Road
St. Leonards on Sea
East Sussex TN38 0QN

Telephone: 01424 720100
Fax: 01424 720323
e-Mail: rveale@studygroup.com
Web: www.studygroup.com/embassyces/english/centres/hastings.asp.

Director: Reg Veale
Welfare and Accommodation Officer: Tina Ballard

Our centre occupies an imposing Victorian building right in a pleasant residential area close to the seafront and the local amenities. It offers excellent modern facilities including a multi-media computer suite and student cafeteria. The centre is home to our International Teacher Training Institute and Executive Centre. We offer general English courses at all levels and vacation programmes for students of 12 years and above.

EF International School of English

Palace Court
White Rock
Hastings
East Sussex TN34 1JP
Telephone: 01424 430156
Fax: 01424 713943
e-Mail: anders.ahlguist@ef.com
lisa.cairns@ef.com
Web: www.ef.com.

Director: Anders Ahlguist
Accommodation Officer: Debbie Barham

EF International School of English offers general and intensive English courses, from beginners to advanced level. Modern facilities centrally located on the seafront. Extensive computer based capacities for optimal learning efficiency.

English For You

25 Wellington Square,
Hastings
East Sussex TN34 1PN
Telephone & Fax: 01424 717320

Director: Fiona Cullen, BA Hons, PGCE TEFL, MA Ling
Accommodation Officer: L Skowronski

Family-run school established in 1988. Situated in a beautiful central square near beach. Courses all year at all levels. Small classes. Emphasis on speaking. Preparation for Cambridge and other public examinations. Course certificate and report. Free personal study advice. 24 hour welfare service. Choice of self-catering or friendly homestay accommodation. Exciting summer free-time programme with wide variety of excursions.

Hastings College (School of English)

The International Department
Archery Road, St Leonards on Sea
East Sussex TN38 0HX
Telephone: 01424 445471
Fax: 01424 424804

Director: Tim Strickland
Accommodation Officer: Sheila Claughton

We provide many different English courses including general, examination, business, computing and summer school. Our International Department is set on lovely grounds and offers good value, effective courses with experienced teachers. There is a great environment to meet friends and our social programme has a variety of cultural day trips and fun nights out. Our excellent facilities include pool and table tennis tables and a self access centre with free email and internet.

Hastings English Language Centre (HELC)

St Helen's Park Road
Hastings
East Sussex TN34 2JW
Telephone: 01424 437048/441549
Fax: (01424) 716442/716450
e-Mail: english@helc.co.uk
Web: www.helc.co.uk.

Director: Mrs P Knight
Accommodation Officer: Mrs K Baker

High quality, general, business and executive courses for serious adult students and professionals. Minimum age 18 for general courses. Small international classes of 5-8 (5-10 in summer) offer a high level of individual attention. Executive courses in small groups with personal 121 tuition focussing on individual training needs. Business courses with 4-6 participants are an ideal introduction to professional English. Excellent location, 2 elegant buildings and modern facilities. Homestay and guest house accommodation selected to suit individual needs is within walking distance of the school.

Mahavis International English Language School

1 York Buildings
Wellington Place
Hastings
TN34 1NN
Telephone: 01424 434885
Fax: 01424 465599
e-Mail: director@mahavis.com
Web: www.mahavis.com
Accommodation Officer: Aizhan Mahavi

Situated right in the town centre, this professional friendly school has a wealth of experience in the successful teaching of English to students from other cultures and language backgrounds. Self Access facilities, a Computer I'lab, and professional native-speaker ELT-qualified teachers are a feature of this family-run school. A full range of general, specialist and examination courses are offered as well as host family accommodation and a full activity programme.

Pinelands Language Centre

114 St Helens Down
Hastings
East Sussex TN34 2AR
Telephone: 01424 421506
Fax: 01424 426787
e-Mail: ann@pinelands.co.uk
Web: www.pinelands.co.uk.

Director: Ann Parsons
Accommodation Officer: Lindsey Beaton

Pinelands Language Centre offers a variety of courses tailored to suit groups and individuals.

Senlac Tours Ltd

Broomhill
Catsfield
Battle
East Sussex TN33 9BA
Telephone: 01424 773280

Director: Angelika Fuller
Accommodation Officer: Joan Shearer

Senlac Tours is a long established company organising both cultural and language trips in eight centres throughout England, Scotland and Ireland, with Hastings being our main centre. We organise transport, channel crossing, accommodation in host families, youth hostels or hotels and programmes for any groups for instance from schools, clubs or tour operators. Our staff speak English, German, Dutch, French and Spanish.

The Ardmore Group

Berkshire College
Berkshire SL6 6QR
Telephone: 01628 8266999
Fax: 01628 829977
e-Mail: morag@theardmoregroup.com

UK Programmes Manager: Ms Morag Anderson
Local Host Family Organiser: Carol Howell
Telephone: 01424 850304
Fax: 01424 851986
e-Mail: travelingtrios@aol.com

YES Education Centre is now part of the Ardmore Group. Many years of experience in organising multi-national student vacation courses in Hastings at Easter, summer and autumn for groups. Each week students receive 20 lessons, two excursions, two sport sessions, one disco, local visits and activities. Carefully selected host families. Qualified teachers and activities staff. Specialists in providing tailor-made courses comprising tuition, excursions, activities, host family accommodation for closed groups. Short stay budget courses and cultural visits for school groups also arranged throughout the year. A wide range of excursions and visits is offered. Host family accommodation provided.

Shane Global Language Centres Hastings Ltd

7 Warrior Square
St. Leonards on Sea
East Sussex TN37 6BA
Telephone: 01424 712000
Fax: 01424 200012
e-Mail: hastings@sgvenglish.com
Web: www.gvenglish.com.

Director: Berwyck Gibbons
Accommodation Officer: Trish Barton

SGV Hastings is a vibrant institution with a family atmosphere located in an impressive Victorian 5 storey terrace overlooking Warrior Square and the seafront. The school is part of a global network which seeks to promote quality and excellence in the world of English language teaching. We offer various courses all of which are tailored to meet the needs of our multi-national students.

STS

97 Sedlescombe Road North
St. Leonards on Sea
TN37 7DS
Telephone: 01424 434860

STS has been running summer language courses in Hastings for students from all over the world since 1958. We offer national, international and intensive courses sold through our sales offices in 22 countries. As well as stimulating our students in the classroom we also offer a full activity programme that allows them to explore Hastings and the surrounding area.

Study Tours

The Chestnuts
Clayhill
Beckley
East Sussex TN31 6SQ

Telephone & Fax: 01797 253502
e-Mail: whitestudytoursltd@supanet.com
Web: www.studytoursuk.co.uk.

Director: Mrs Debbie White

Operating for more than 25 years in the South East, we offer tailor-made visits to suit all requirements for all ages. Personal service is assured.

White Rock Mansions

9 White Rock Road
Hastings
East Sussex TN34 1LE
Telephone & Fax: 01424 460510
e-Mail: ht166@aol.com

Director: S Abeling
Accommodation Officer: D Barham

A four star group hostel offering superb accommodation for school and youth groups. Situated in a quiet position close to Hastings town centre and the seafront. Many rooms offer excellent sea views and all have ensuite facilities. There is a choice of home cooked meal options to suit your individual group needs. Conference/meeting rooms available.

NATIONAL AND GLOBAL CRISES.

Langage schools, in common with all industries dependent on travel, are vulnerable to national and global crises. Early in my own venture into the overseas student industy in the mid-1990s, Hastings was exposed to some adverse publicity about a local victim of the condition necrotizing fasciitis, "the flesh eating disease" as the tabloids ghoulishly headlined the plight of the Hastings man. Suddenly, in the way of such things there were cases brought to light in other UK locations. This news item appeared in the Milan media and was picked up by the parents of our students, set for departure to Hastings. Panic ensued and I was obliged to consult my GP, who assured me that there were no more and no less cases of this dreadful disease either locally or nationally than in previous years. One language school owner said he became afraid to listen the news at times, wondering what new catastrophe would strike and affect his business.

Britain later suffered the BSE crisis, when the fear of eating infected beef either kept the students at home or made them afraid to eat, even seemingly innnocuous dishes like fruit jelly were suspect. But much worse was to come. In February 2001 a Foot and Mouth epidemic began, which ultimately resulted in millions of hooved livestock being slaughtered all over the UK. Dramatic TV and newspaper images of mountainous bonfires of dead animals went worldwide. Bans were placed on visitors to famous rural attractions and countryside walkers were limited to footpaths. This had a disastrous effect on tourism, including the overseas student business.

When the World Trade Centre came under terrorist atack on 11th September 2001, with its resultant effect on air travel, things became even more catastrophic for the already beleagured language schools of Hastings, as the following Hastings and St Leonards articles reveal:

TERRORISM FEAR SCARES OFF FOREIGN STUDENTS 12th October 2001

'Foreign students are being scared away from Hastings by the US terror attacks - dealing a savage blow to the town's economy. One of the best-known and long-established language schools is to close. And there are serious fears that could be just the first victim in a business that brings millions of pounds into the town each year. The closure of the EF International Language School will be felt by traders throughout Hastings and also by hundreds of local people who rely heavily on income from providing accommodation for the students. Council marketing Chief Kevin Boorman said that he hopes it will not mean the total collapse of the language business in the town. He fears a serious downfall over the whole sector for long-haul students - there have already been 30 to 50 per cent cancellations around the world. Mr Boorman hopes the town will pick up more European business but he could not say the loss of the long-haul would be compensated by this. The EF International Language School which takes mature students all the year round will close its doors at Christmas, although EF Language Travel seasonal courses for younger students will continue. The closure of the year-round international school at Warrior Square is one of the far-reaching economic effects of the terrorist attack. It has already impacted on airline companies, holiday business and tourism generally. Language schools are a huge business in Hastings - there are 26 registered schools, possibly another 15 unregistered, bringing in 30,000-35,000 students (plus 10,000 at the unregistered schools) providing income for host families. The director of EF International School of English, told the Observer: "It's a big

decision for our company and it's a big loss. It is such a shock for everyone. It will hit the 18 staff but it's not known how many jobs will go. Following the tragic events in America on 11th September and the consequent downturn we have experienced in the demand for language study programmes in England, sadly, we have had to make the very difficult decision to consolidate and down-size our operations in Hastings." The school has been a prominent part of the local language school scene since 1974 and was the company's first year-round teaching centre in England. But it's now the company's smallest school in the UK; EF will continue to offer year-round courses at their schools in Brighton, Bournemouth, London and Cambridge.'

(EF has returned to Hastings since this report was published)

FOREIGN LANGUAGE SCHOOL CLOSES 23rd November 2001

'A second foreign language school has closed in a matter of weeks - because students were scared away from Hastings by the foot-and-mouth crisis. The Centre for English Studies at Caple-ne-Ferne in Albany Road, lost half its trade following negative publicity about the disease around the world. It is a second disaster to the town in a month after EF International Language School announced its closure because of travel fears after the US terror attacks. The sale of the 18th century building could be Hastings' first million-pound residential property. Mr Dan Tranter, who has run the school since 1993, was forced to close after parties of students aged between eight and 19 from across the world cancelled, while other groups arrived smaller than planned. He said: "It's a disaster. We have overcome the BSE crisis which reduced groups coming from France, the strength of the pound for three or four years and the collapse of the Russian economy. We survived all this only to fall foul of foot-and-mouth. Five permanent staff and nine other people have lost their jobs. It is all down to the terrible press about the disease across the world. I knew there would be tough months ahead when a group of students from the Ukraine cancelled just days before they were due to arrive in March. If people are sending their child to England they want to be sure they will be safe. Lots of children were terrified of eating the food when they arrived. We educated them and they soon began to enjoy eggs and

bacon. But the fear was still there." Mr Tranter applied to Sussex Enterprise for emergency grants and funding to prevent his business going under, but no money was left. He had no intention of selling after a huge outlay of £30,000 to update the 92-bedroom property, installing new showers and a play area this year. "We were building for the future. But retirement has come early and it would make a fantastic home." Marketing chief Kevin Boorman said: "We regret the demise of a well-established school such as this and we are putting all our efforts into attracting foreign language students to the town." Mark Rush, of Rush, Witt and Wilson estate agents said that a number of offers for the former London Transport convalescence home have already been received.'

It may interest those who study the fortunes of local, well-known buildings that Caple-ne-Ferne was eventually sold to the owner of the Warrior Square Adelphi Hotel, home to scores of asylum seekers, with a view to using the former language school similarly, for 71 new arrivals. Local residents were in an uproar, they had previously delayed the opening of the former language school by many months with a flood of objections. There proved to be a problem about the change of use of the building from a school to a hostel for the asylum seekers. The new owner set up language courses in an attempt to fulfil the conditions but this failed and the building passed into new hands in August 2004, to serve as a drug users' rehabilitation centre, run on the principles laid down by L Ron Hubbard, founder of the Church of Scientology.

Further local protest brought the assurance by the centre management that everyone entering the premises had left drugs behind and if found with drugs they would be thrown out. "We are trying to rehabilitate former drug users, to help them learn valuable social skills, which will keep them off drugs and help them become model citizens. The 24 staff at the Albany Road centre will aim to eliminate drug dependency through a regime of 10-hour study programmes, coupled with a regime of exercise, guided nutrition and toxin-expunging sauna sessions."
This, one supposes, is how the change of use barrier was overcome.

THIRD FOREIGN LANGUAGE SCHOOL FOLDS 20th December 2001

'A third foreign language school has closed in Hastings - thanks to the foot-and-mouth crisis. Majors School of English, in Warrior Square, was forced to shut its doors after a massive 250 students failed to travel. Cancellations coincided with expensive re-decorating which meant the owners struggled to keep up with bills. Just three classrooms and an administrative office remain, as the centre seeks new premises to rent in the New Year. Staff will continue to train Indian nurses for the NHS. It is a crippling blow to the town. Major's School, who will lay off two staff, said: "This year has been terrible. We had three cancelled bookings after foot-and-mouth which dealt us a terrible blow. Students add a huge income for many families, particularly those on low income". It could hurt the local community and have a knock-on effect on the town. But while three schools have closed, Embassy CES and Elysian Cultural Studies said business is booming. The principal of Embassy, said: "We are doing well. Obviously the events of 11th September didn't help and we did have cancellations, particularly from Argentina. But there has been a surge of business from Russia and there will be two or three groups at least coming immediately after the New Year, from Brazil and South America. We have the same number of people as last year and if you count the groups, we have more." The owner of Elysian said: "It is absolutely first-rate. We only take students from Germany who are still travelling here and loving Hastings." She added that Battle and Rye also benefit as students travel there on day trips. The director of Hastings Language School said: "I am not getting over optimistic, but considering the strength of the pound, the after - effects of the BSE crisis, foot-and-mouth and the September 11 attacks, it's not looking too bad." Not all schools share the same optimism. The director of Language Services Worldwide said that he was unsure how good business would be until next year. He added: "We have got bookings, but from Poland only. Foot-and-mouth was a huge factor, particularly with students from Italy who did not want to travel to Britain. They are a huge market to Hastings. But some groups will come over from France and Spain for Easter." The owner of English for You said that business has been slower but he could also not tell until next year.'

HOPES OF STUDENT BOOM 11th April 2002

'It seems many students eager to study English in Hastings have put fears over foot and mouth, BSE, and September 11 behind them. The student business brings an amazing £35million into the town and boosts not only the schools but shops, eating places, taxi firms and host families. Currently at the Embassy CES School at White Rock, there is a group of 25 from Thailand, and other groups from Switzerland and Austria, with other, long-term students making 200 in all. The school's principal said: "We have had a busy springtime and generally speaking things are looking up. Bookings are significantly higher than this time last year. We are looking at a fairly busy summer as long as there is nothing like foot and mouth or September 11. It doesn't seem to be an issue with the Europeans now or with Far Eastern students and nor those from South America, which is another big market for us." Hastings Council marketing manager Kevin Boorman said: "I am optimistic the town can get back to the student numbers of a few years ago of 35,000 to 40,000. While numbers from Japan are down, it's a more buoyant picture with European students. Although business from Germany is slightly down there is a 20 per cent increase in the number from France, with the rest of Europe holding its own. We are particularly pleased with the situation from France. We have worked hard to break into the French market. We are encouraged that things have gone so well. We are continuing to work with the language schools to make sure students thoroughly enjoy their stay and get the most out of their visit to Hastings.'

CHAPTER EIGHT

WILL THE UMBRELLA NEED ME?

It seems appropriate to close the story of overseas students in Hastings by bringing it up to date with comments from the students of 2006. When I began this book I thought how fortunate they are, making their visit during a time of peace, unlike those who had to flee home to France in August 1939, when war was imminent. But on Thursday 10th August 2006 I was sharply reminded that the world is even now engaged in a war. We woke that day to hear that British airports were in chaos; an alleged plot by terrorists to blow up British passenger flights in mid-air had been discovered and stringent and time-consuming emergency security checks on outgoing passengers were underway at all UK airports.

The previous week I had been to see the Director of Studies of a Hastings language school, to ask if he would allow me to set an essay competition for his older students, in which I would ask them to write their impressions of Hastings. A copy of my book, Letters to Hannah was to be the prize. The DoS agreed to my proposition. It was some time since I had been inside a language school and exposed to the frantic activity and chaos created by hordes of students milling about in the rambling, converted Victorian hotels and apartment buildings that serve as education centres in the town.

Kay Green wrote the following piece about her TEFL experiences;

'It takes a special kind of character to function in the chaotic, high-pressure atmosphere of a large summer-school without killing anyone or having a heart- attack. One such who made quite an impression on me was – let's call him Lars – a slight, dark-haired, bespectacled philosopher of a man, with the quiet resilience a Scandinavian upbringing sometimes produces. I met him at the sweltering height of a busy summer. I was between jobs, but that's no problem for a TEFL teacher in July. Freelancing and fill-ins were already keeping me somewhat busier than I wanted to be when Lars called and said he was

urgently in need of an Assistant Director of Studies (ADoS). This was a Tuesday. I said I'd be available the following Monday for interview. He said, 'come and have lunch. You can start on Monday.'

I arrived at the language school at lunchtime, amongst a babbling mass of teenagers. I pushed and excuse-me'd through the dark, imposing hallway of the huge Victorian apartment building which had been adapted some years before to house a summer-school for several hundred students. I followed hastily erected signs up a couple of flights of stairs and across a couple more hallways. There were posters, bags, jackets, suitcases, teenagers, books, shouts, tears and laughter everywhere. Somehow, the lofty stairwell held onto its Victorian seaside reserve, and absorbed most of the din. In a pre-fabricated, panelled office I found three receptionists womanning three flashing computers and four ringing telephones. Between calls one managed to throw me some clues as to the whereabouts of Lars. I began my search of the thronged corridors. On my second time around, I began giving directions to any students who happened to ask about places I'd seen on my travels through the labyrinth. On my third time around I noticed the canteen, so I put my head in at the reception office and said I'd go start lunch, and Lars could come and find me.

The huge, sunshine-yellow canteen echoed with all the activities of a study-centre, plus lunch, plus kids on holiday. I was still being asked for directions at the rate of about one lost soul per minute. By the time Lars found me I was checking someone's homework for them. He smiled sweetly at me, put his head in his hands and took a fifteen-second nap, then looked up and said – "what can I do for you?" I said, "you said you needed an ADoS here." "God, yes" he said. "Actually, I could do with four - oh, I forgot to get myself coffee." The coffee – and the interview – lasted approximately three minutes.

The school I had worked in for most of my TEFL life was a year-round exam centre – incredibly organised and staid in comparison to what I was seeing here. However, curiosity coupled with an instinctive liking for Lars, led me to accept this job. I stood up to leave but he asked me to find the acting ADoS and have an 'orientation session.' It meant a swift re-organising of my schedule, but I did so. I got in about half-an-hour of learning the computer system, and was then asked to sign for and organise a delivery of books. That didn't sound too complicated until I realised we were talking about a large lorry-load. The books – booklets really – were part of a system running from one to three hundred or something. They proved to be a specially designed system to give step-by-step instructions to students and teacher who have never met before and may never meet again. There was nowhere to put them and no system for allocating them. I grabbed a couple of bystanders – students I assume – to help me unwrap them and stack them in some sort of order along a wall, and announced a self-service system for teachers to pick them up.

That was as far as I got with orientation before a student came to me with a tale of a teacher-less class on the top floor. There was no sign of the ADoS who had been 'orienting' me. All investigations leading to a complete blank, I left the books to mind themselves and plunged into the afflicted classroom to give a somewhat off-the-cuff lesson. I found Lars in a corridor at five o' clock, drew breath to report on my day, got a sad smile and a 'thanks, see you on Monday.' Monday morning is at best organised chaos in any language school. New arrivals are coming in from all the corners of the globe, trailing with them all kinds of expectations and all the problems of first-time travellers. In this temporary, high-density summer-school it was unbelievable. Every large hall was full of students taking level tests. The reception office and the Director of Studies office were packed with anxious and tearful admin problems, and the staff room was full of newly signed-up teachers yelling, 'Who? Where? How? Which room? How many...?'

I found the acting ADoS trying to answer two telephones and a mobile, whilst fielding a ceaseless dribble of urgent emails and ignoring a queue of agitated students. I grabbed a roster and started dealing with the queue. Finding answers to their questions was my voyage of discovery. Behind and around me, I heard Lars and his ADoS arranging tutors for students who were on exam courses, booking day-trips, setting up activities. To my amazement, it appeared that despite the chaos, learning was going on and fun was being had. This time I did a full four hours work before discovering a teacher-less class and changing hats again. I was actually heading for reception to find out why the fire alarms kept blipping but decided to go sort out the class *first, get them working on something, then come back to reception. Running on automatic pilot, I got talking to the class, got them talking to each other, and put together the lead-in to a conversation-development activity on the board.*

Meanwhile half my brain was attending to the continuing strange noises coming from the fire alarm and the fact that I didn't know who my fire-report officer was. The other half of my brain was assessing the permanent job I'd been offered that morning and weighing up my options in the light of the fact that my daughter was nine months and two weeks pregnant. (I had warned Lars of my possible sudden disappearance, but wasn't too sure that his passing remark "yeah that's cool," counted as having heard it.) The doors burst open and another class began to flow into our room. I leaped into the aisle to field them and as I did so the fire alarm went off in earnest. I glanced at the French windows at the back of the room bearing the sign FIRE EXIT. I knew they opened onto a long and rickety walkway. I didn't know how to get from there to the street. I pushed through the students who had invaded my room, wrenched the classroom door open and saw Lars loping along the corridor outside "Which way out!" I yelled. "Front door!" he replied, and was gone. I began the herding process. "Leave that, leave that, don't worry - this way - follow Mari - don't run." By the time we reached the stairs, we had flowed into half a dozen other groups. One look down the stairwell told me the hallway was blocked solid. My training from the previous school had taught me that there is no such thing as a false alarm. As I continued to coral my class, my mind was going over possible alternative exits and searching for simple ways of explaining the route to the students. Meanwhile my body was yelling, "I'm going to faint! Fall down the stairs! Die!! FAIL MY STUDENTS!!!" Fortunately, things began to move. We reached the lower hallway, and emerged onto the street. The building expelled the horde of students in an avalanche which spilled along the path in both directions and into the road in a widening crowd. As each teacher exploded onto the street, they leaped into the road and started trying to direct the flow.

At the corner stood Lars, the rush-hour traffic spinning past inches from his bottom, as he did his impression of a human crash-barrier. With one hand he was waving to a fire-engine hurtling towards us from the middle distance, with the other he absent-mindedly patted the shoulder of a small Eastern European boy who was trying to ask him about question four of his homework. Round the corner, the acting ADoS was engaged in a screaming match with some local kids who had decided that if there was a fire, it would be useful to chuck bottlefuls of water at the students in the street. Ten minutes or so later I had assembled my class round the corner, reported them all to be alive and well, told them to go home, and left the scene.

The next day I told Lars I'd be leaving at the end of the week or when my daughter gave birth – whichever happened first. He was philosophical about it, told me to come back when I could. The next day I became a grandmother.'

I gave the students who entered my essay competition a set of prompts and questions as follows:

What do you think of Hastings as a resort to visit?

Mention its places of entertainment and visitor attractions.

What is your opinion of our local transport system, shops and restaurants?

Write something about your host family, British food and way of life.

Have you been treated unkindly or rudely in public or subjected to street violence?

Feel free to write about any topic I have not mentioned.

I had hoped for quite a high number of entries, forgetting that these were older students with a serious aim in studying English and my essay competition may have been a distraction from more important work. Therefore I was grateful for the essays that were submitted. To avoid repetition I have not included all references to local attractions, unless they are pertinent. Where practical I have kept to the original language of the essays and honoured the frankness of the students' observations, even if they are damning at times. Host families are not named.

Germany: Patrick, Age 20

Hastings is small nice town. I like all old thinks, old buildings, old cars, old furniture, antique and young women. The English people are kind and gregarious in the pubs. The go out possibilities are big. My guest family are very kindly and courteous. They wait the dinner and eat when I come. They always eat with me and talk about different things. All the evening I go out or watch videos with my guest father.

Country of origin name and age unknown.

I think that many host families are very much used to hosting students and it's not amazing for many of them to receive a new guest each half month. This fact makes families behave as if they are running a hostel. I mean, we want to live the English style of life at home as well and we have to do an extra effort when we arrive home to integrate in the family. From my point of view Hastings has got the appropriate resources to be a big resort but it isn't, because of the lack of enjoying point of view in people and public institutions. It's difficult to enjoy a town that has a lack of entertainment places. The pubs are empty of people, is not warm and friendly.

Russia: Alexandra, Age 19

I think that Hastings is a good place for those who are tired of big cities and want to spend their holidays in peace and quiet. It is good to be back to a small town after long day-trips to London and Stonehenge. The only problem is there are no direct trains to famous places in Britain, like Oxford, Cambridge or Canterbury.

However, there are lots of bars and clubs and if you want to dance the whole night go to Fluid. But the place I recommend is French. It's a bar where you can drink a tasty and cheap beer in the evening and nice coffee in the day.

What else to see? Alexandra Park but it's like in every town and city. If you cook yourself Morrison's is the cheapest shop, where you can find everything. Cinemas they show too much ads before the film and it's annoying.

My host family is really wonderful. The hostess is a cooking wizard. Myself I've decided to buy a British national cookery book. Besides I took some recipes from her. She is happy to tell me stories and recommend some places to see.

Hastings is safe to walk; people are ready to help you find the way. I am completely satisfied because I live not far from the centre and beach and most interesting places. My friends tell me that in the edges of the town the situation is completely different.

Switzerland: Thomas, Age 22

The buses of Hastings are terrible. Specially in the evenings and Sunday there are too few buses. They are never on time, how could they be when the time table shows the same time for ten different bus stops? Sometimes the bus driver just doesn't stop, although there are a lot of people at the station and some make a sign with their hands. Or even when I press the button in the bus I cannot be sure that the bus will finally stop. But I think that the lines are well spread so you won't have to walk far to the next stop wherever you are.

The churches here are wonderful. Everywhere there are churches. Also the old town of Hastings, St Leonards Warrior Square and the castle or what is remaining of it are worth seeing. There are some very nice pubs in Hastings for example the Havelock and the London Trader. But the Fluid Disco is not nice at all. The music is too loud and you can only hear the noise. I think the people here really like fighting, nearly everyday I can see a fight. I don't like that, it seems to be dangerous here. Altogether I like Hastings but not very much.

My host family is really great. The food is fine and they often talk to me. I feel welcome in their home and I could feel they are enjoying the presence of foreign students in their home.

Spain: Jose Antonio, Age 28
When I was looking for a place to do my English course during the summer I wanted a place with sea, beach and not very big. I wanted to go walking everywhere. I am not keen of busy cities when I am on holidays. Hastings has got these features and besides is one of the cheaper cities in the area.

Some days after I arrived in Hastings I noticed that this town is quiet but more than I thought. I mean from my point of view Hastings is not using all its potential. This town could reach to be a great resort. It has got good transport ways specially by train, a nearby airport and it's located only two hours away from London, has good weather, a wide beach. The coaches that serve Hastings and the surrounding areas provide enough service. The frequency could be higher and the timetables are chaotic.

Germany: Male, Age 19.

The writer of this contribution chose an efficiently Teutonic pro/con list-method to present his opinions, from which I have extracted:

The beach is good; the town has a quiet atmosphere with a lot of nature. Many hills, strenuous to walk.

The local transport is obvious and clear but expensive in comparison to other countries.

The shops are cheap for books, shoes or belts but the business hours are not good. Restaurants are good but expensive.

Food. Tasty, if you like a lot of rice.

People are friendly and most of the time they are in a good mood. Sometimes you miss the safety because it's dangerous to wear your camera obviously with you.

My host family is very friendly and open-hearted, always trying to integrate you but they sometimes seem to be bit backward.

Saudi Arabia: Female, Age 19.

I think that Hastings has very few places of attraction. It is a little city or town, for me there aren't many places that I can meet my friends after school and have cup of coffee or something. There's just night clubs at night and for me I can't go to these places because people will

139

be drunk there. For me I can't wait until the weekend to go to somewhere else. Hastings has a nice beach. Hastings is very dirty. About the local transport, it is very expensive. The taxis charge you more than five pounds for less than five minutes. The buses are also expensive - we are students! The shops are not very good, well I can't buy anything here except for souvenirs. There are very few places where I would go for eat, for example The Italian Way and Subway but other restaurants I don't like to go there because it smells and the food there has no taste.

About my host family. They are fine but becoz they are just a couple I don't have the chance to talk to them except for dinner but there are times that I feel I interrupt them, of course I don't do that! Also I think that 4 pounds per washing is expensive. They also place or put the plates or bowls for dogs with our plates in the dishwasher. We told them about that but they said that the hot water in the dishwasher is enough to remove all the germs from these bowls. I have never tried the British food but generally my host family cooks well.

We have our own room what we asked for with hot water in it. I think we are fine. I don't know if you want me to write about just my host family and other host families becoz I have heard a lot of horrible stories about them from my friends here and some of them starve them. Even if they are just 15 or 30 minutes late for dinner! Which I think is not fair becoz sometimes the buses here don't come the right time, they are late and sometimes they never show up. A few times this has happened to me.

I think the people here are very helpful they like to help people although they are not friendly at all, even my host family. They're very strict with their things. I think they are ignorant. People here don't care they way you look no matter where you come from. They think that's it's not of their concern - or so think –which is a good thing. People in shops are very welcoming and I like that. I don't know much about public so I think that's it.

Saudi Arabia: Nizar, (male) age 17.

I have a good experience in Hastings. I think that it is a good town to study in because it is quiet and there isn't so many people but it is good to visit Hastings. There is specific things to do and see in Hastings, You can go to old town you can go and see museum or to White Rock and see a play. Or if you like dancing you can go to the disco in town centre. My opinion about the local transport the bus is cheap and easy to get around Hastings, You can take a taxi but it is more expensive than buses. If you want you can rent a car. In Hastings there is so many shops and markets and it is always sale and there is also many restaurant and cafe next to the shops.

About my host family. I like my host family and I am very happy with them there is very friendly women and three student who is from Poland and one Saudi Arabia. The famous British food is fish and chips. The way of life is easier than life in Saudi. The women has more freedom. She can live independently. I have not been treated rudely or unkindly in Hastings. The people in Hastings have been helpful every time.

Kim age, gender and national origin unknown.

Hastings is a place where you can relax and enjoy yourself at your own speed. It's also a place where you can enjoy the stony beach, ancient museum, nice shops, west and east sights. For me Hastings is like a tranquilizer. Everything seems so calm. It is another life. All the shops and different places are closed very early. It is good if you are from a busy and noisy city.

What about food? Honestly when I arrived I was shocked because almost all the food was disgusting. Traditionally meal include the sandwich, fish and chips, pies, beef, pork, potatoes and one other vegetable. Usually I prefer healthy food but here it's difficult that's why almost every day I attend sport centre and I like it. I can say Hastings has a wonderful gym.

I am lucky because I don't know any host family better than mine. They welcome and hospitable, incredible and terrific. My family consist of Jemma 27 years old and Timothy. Jemma is young maybe that is why she can understand me very well. I love her. She is considerate and cooks great dinners. My family is really nice. They always help me when I have some problems. Recently we sat in the kitchen and Jemma was showing me their married photos. It was unforgettable because I have never seen wedding like this. I thought that it would be difficult to understand English people but no. I can speak on almost every subject. I used to live with one French girl she almost didn't know English it was difficult to speak with her. But now I live with another French. She is kind and considerate. At once we became friends.

In the evening we usually go to the beach that's why I have lot of photos and videos. It's incredible to see the sunset in Hastings. By the evening the water as a rule is hotter than in the afternoon. Trust me, it's really true! What about my school? Very, very friendly teachers. They understand everything. Especially I want to tell about Mark, Daniel, Nicola and Gitana.

Russian: Probably female, age and name unknown

This is my first visit in that country. When I arrived in Hastings I was very surprising because it is a small city. I live in Moscow and I got used to live in big, noise city with intensive lifestyle. However, I like Hastings, particularly the old part. I like to walk in the old town. There are many small calm streets there. All the houses aren't high, mostly they has from 2 to 4 floors and a lot of them are very old. I think that they has theyself a story.

Every day I enjoy fresh sea air and the sight of the sea. Hastings is located on a hill or mountains, its very beautiful but every day I walk down to school and its easy but after I have to go walk up to home about 30 minutes and its hard for me but very usefully.

I don't like a weather in England because every day when I wake up I think about what kind of dress I can clother? And will the umbrella need me or won't? It is so because in the morning the weather is cold and windy, but afternoon – almost always sunshine. I stay in Hastings not so far from our school. But I am not distress oneself about it because I am glad and very happy stay at my host family. This family consist them from 3 persons. They are very kind and friendly, communicative and funny! Almost every evening their daughter plays different music on the piano. She has a beautiful voice! They are a good teachers and if I don't understand something in some situation they are always explain me and help me learn English. Their daughter is very good guide and once she showed us Brighton city.

A lot of student complains to some food in England but I like it because my host family cooks a different dish from some beef, fish, vegetables every day. It's very tasty and they makes delicious coffee in the morning! I tried also some different buns. For example Chelsea bun and some biscuit. It's traditional food in England and it was tasty. Also there are a lot of places where you can fast and cheap eat.

I don't like the shopping in Hastings. There are not famous brand of closes in Hastings. A little shop has some closes of a good quality. In spite of this I like to look in jewellery shops because there are some interesting and beautiful objects.

I cannot speak anything about a bus because I didn't use it. But I was using some train when I visited London. I liked the train it was moving very punctually and were very clean and comfortable. I think this sort of transport is safety and acceptable. Sometimes I used a taxi and it was not too expensive in comparison with evening service in Moscow.

A lot of people are very kind and friendly in Hastings. If you need some help they are can help you. People in the shops or the restaurants laugh with you and they are very honest. Some drivers are very polite and if you need to cross the street they are stop always. It was a big surprising for me because in Moscow it isn't happen never! The teachers in school are very nice and diligent and if you have some problems they try to help you and explain some items again and again. That's great! This is all just my impression.

The winner of the competition, chosen by her tutor

Germany: Helen Age 25.

I visited Hastings for the first time and I think it's a nice town with an old history. Hastings is in any case a worthwhile resort, because it has some interesting attractions. One of these is the Hasting Castle which gives a marvellous view of whole old town and the sea. Close to the hill along the beach you can find other attractions like the Fishermen's Museum and the Sea Life centre. It is a must for lovers of history. Unfortunately the pier was closed and I couldn't enjoy the view over the sea. Great places for entertainment are the cinema, the White Rock Theatre and the Stables Theatre. Unfortunately, I still have not found an opportunity to visit these.

Worthwhile of mention is the club 'The Crypt' because it is a nice location for young people. I can't say about the transport system because I didn't need to use it. But for the outside of Hastings the train was quite useful and cheap. There are a great variety of shops and restaurants. For students and young people for example Subway, McDonald and KFC are quite useful. If you have a bit more time I recommend the restaurant Cosmos Chinese restaurant with the offer to eat as much as you can for a cheap price.

I can say just the best about my host family. On my first day I got a very kindly welcome and a short walk up the hill. I got my own room and I am allowed to use the TV and DVD. My host family cooks every evening different but very good food. Even my own wishes were interesting to them. I absolutely dislike the British tradition of fish and chips (to fat) or traditional breakfast. I am very glad about their healthy attitude of food. So there are a lot of salad, fresh cooked food and fruit. The dinners always take place with the whole family (as far as possible) and we talk a lot.

Particularly their daughter is very attentive and spends a lot of time with me (us) She guided us through Brighton with lunch at their father's family and a guide through London: she also introduced her friends to me (us). My host family is a very open minded family and their way of life is similar to mine. One difference: no one goes to school before 9.00am. Fortunately I haven't had any experience with violence or unkindly behaviour up to now. I will visit my host family again in the near future.

As the work of researching this book drew to a close I had a conversation with the now retired owner of a language school. We talked about the future of the overseas student industry in Hastings. He said that he feared that as far as the Eastern European market is concerned the UK may lose out to Australia and New Zealand, as these countries are not much further from Eastern Europe than are the British Isles. He also said that the requirements of today's students are more sophisticated and that nowadays they would expect an Internet connection in the host family's home.

What is clear from the students' essays is that wherever the student goes the most important thing is the welcome and treatment they receive from their host family. As this book is dedicated to the host families of Hastings and St Leonards, it seems appropriate to end it with a short letter that I received in August 2006, from a lady who wishes to be known as Mrs A.

Dear Mrs Seymour.

I am a mum who brought up three sons. For 11 years I was also a dinner lady at our local school. I loved having children around, no matter what age they were so when my sons left home I missed them sorely. Then I was widowed in my mid-fifties and I felt I needed to fill the emptiness in my life. I was approached about having students and I felt I would be able to welcome them into my home; being on my own I decided to have girls.

What a pleasure they all were. I have hosted 12 students, all of whom came from Italy; some of them came back to stay with me several times. Every one of them was delightful and they became my family. They were very trustworthy and I had no hesitation in giving them a key but I never went to bed until they were home.

To get on with young people one has to understand their needs, welcome them with open arms and do everything possible while they are in your home to look after them.

If you have never been a student host I suggest you give it a try. What you give to them will be returned to you in abundance.

BIBLIOGRAPHY

'Taking in Students, How to make your spare room pay,' by Rosemary Bartholomew published in 1996.

The book is now out of print but can be obtained from Hastings Public Library ISBN 1-85703-323-X Lib item ref 02562768.

The History of Hastings Grammar School Edited by J R Conisbee and J Manwaring Baines. A copy is held in Hastings Public Library.

Group Profiles by John Dunstar, ELAC Principal.

The Police Operation Columbus website.

The Hastings and St Leonards Observer archive and recent editions.

Herstmonceux Castle website.

Letters from Lavender Cottage

by Victoria Seymour

Hastings in WWII and Austerity

A collection of recently discovered letters, posted from Hastings to Canada between 1942 and 1955, inspired Victoria Seymour to compile a part-biography of their writer, Emilie Crane.

In her retirement, Emilie shared a house in Hastings, England, with her two friends, Clare and Edith and their much-loved cat, James. The almost one hundred letters Emilie sent to her Canadian cousins were initially of thanks for the food parcels they had supplied to the Lavender Cottage household in WWII and throughout the following years of harsh austerity. The letters also detail the lively and kind-hearted Emilie Crane's domestic and personal life and follow the joint fortunes of the three ageing women.

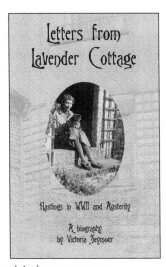

Victoria Seymour has rounded the story by adding contemporary national, local and autobiographical material. "Letters From Lavender Cottage" is a touching, human story with an informative narrative.

ISBN: 0-9543901-0-5   www.victoriaseymour.com

Letters to Hannah

written & compiled by Victoria Seymour

WWII Recollections
of Hastings & South East England

Letters to Hannah looks at WWII on the Home Front through the eyes of those who lived in Hastings and South East England from September 1939 to December 1945. It also enlarges on the historical background covered in its companion book, Letters from Lavender Cottage.

Letters to Hannah visits the lives of ordinary people, who endured extraordinary times. Among many others is the account of a Battle lad, born in a cottage beside the famous 1066 battlefield. Aged fifteen he enlisted as a Home Guard, the youngest member in the country at that time, a Hastings, wartime milk delivery girl details her working and family life under fire and a young first aid volunteer highlights the horrors of bomb and machine gun attacks on civilians. 'Letters to Hannah' is rich in anecdotes and information on food rationing and shortages, the blackout, air raids, population evacuation and civil defence. The book provides a moving and factual account of wartime Hastings, the town which features in the ITV, WWII detective fiction series, Foyle's War.

Victoria Seymour links this, her second WWII social history, with a series of autobiographical letters to the future, describing her war-troubled childhood to her newborn, 21st century granddaughter, Hannah. Extracts from Letters to Hannah were included in the BBC Radio 4 history series, The Archive Hour, in July 2003.

ISBN: 0-9543901-1-3   www.victoriaseymour.com

Court in the Act

written & compiled by Victoria Seymour

Crime and Policing in WWII Hastings
Foreword by Ann Widdecombe M.P.

Victoria Seymour's Court in the Act, which completes her trilogy, concentrates on the work of the police force, the magistrates' and other courts in WWII Hastings. As the effects of war took hold, there was hardly any aspect of home front life that was not controlled by some Government Act, Regulation or Order, putting even more pressure on already overworked police officers.

There passed before the courts a parade of 'spies', aliens, pacifists, looters, wartime racketeers and small-time criminals. Added to these were thousands of usually law-abiding people who found themselves in court for flouting often not properly understood laws. Sentences were handed down that sounded like something out of 19th Century history: A fine for stealing one onion from an allotment, a few apples from a tree or vegetable peelings from a dustbin or a month in prison for allowing light to escape from behind a curtain.

Meanwhile, the formidable Government Enforcers stalked the land incognito, seeking to trap unwary traders and citizens and bring them to justice. Police Court reports from the period 1939 to 1945 give an insight into a little discussed aspect of WWII. 'Vigilant', The Hastings and St Leonards Observer 1940s columnist, provides a background, with comment on the foibles and morals of a seaside town under fire.

Fact met fiction, when in 2004 Victoria Seymour was asked by Greenlit Productions, who film Foyle's War, the WWII detective television drama set in Hastings, to assist in re-creating a Hastings' wartime magistrates' court for series three.

ISBN: 0-9543901-2-1   www.victoriaseymour.com

The Long Road to Lavender Cottage

written & compiled by Victoria Seymour

The now famous occupant of Lavender Cottage, Emilie Crane, returns, to let us back into her life and the daily doings of her neighbours on the Ridge. What was the truth about the supposed nudist colony opposite Lavender Cottage? Was the guest house close by really a haven for left wing agitators and a bolt hole for a scandalous occultist, Aleister Crowley?

Victoria Seymour has meticulously researched the background and history of a period and place that was peopled not just by locals leading ordinary lives but by notable figures from the worlds of literature, religion, the arts, healing, politics and entertainment, including Joanna Lumley.

We are given glimpses into the Ridge's former large Victorian houses, cottages, farms, institutions and businesses and the lives of their occupants in peace time and war. The Long Road to Lavender Cottage also reveals dramatic events in Emilie Crane's daily life that she was not able to write about in her wartime letters, for fear of the government censor.

ISBN: 0-9543901-4-8   www.victoriaseymour.com